Engaging Students Using Cooperative Learning

Motivate your students and create an engaging classroom environment with the time-tested strategies in this book. Drawing on over 35 years of experience, author and consultant John D. Strebe offers a wealth of advice for teachers who want to encourage collaboration and team learning among students of all grade levels. This expanded second edition includes activities and examples across the subject areas, as well as new reproducible tools for classroom use. Topics include…

- Building enthusiasm and increasing student development with games, mini competitions, and team projects.
- Implementing new seating arrangements that promote discussion and participation.
- Keeping students engaged during lectures and presentations.
- Facilitating group work by organizing students into teams based on academic skills and personal traits.
- And more!

John D. Strebe taught secondary mathematics for 38 years in the Maryland public schools. He conducts workshops for teachers across the country, providing instruction on setting up a cooperative and engaging classroom.

T0386141

Other Eye On Education Books Available from Routledge
(www.routledge.com/eyeoneducation)

Battling Boredom, Part 1
99 Strategies to Spark Student Engagement
Bryan Harris

Battling Boredom, Part 2
Even More Strategies to Spark Student Engagement
Bryan Harris and Lisa Bradshaw

75 Quick and Easy Solutions to Common Classroom Disruptions
Bryan Harris and Cassandra Goldberg

Creating a Classroom Culture That Supports the Common Core
Teaching Questioning, Conversation Techniques, and Other Essential Skills
Bryan Harris

Motivating Struggling Learners:
10 Ways to Build Student Success
Barbara R. Blackburn

Rigor is Not a Four-Letter Word, 2nd Edition
Barbara R. Blackburn

Rigor and Assessment in the Classroom
Barbara R. Blackburn

Classroom Instruction from A to Z, 2nd Edition
Barbara R. Blackburn

The Flexible ELA Classroom:
Practical Tools for Differentiated Instruction in Grades 4–8
Amber Chandler

Passionate Learners, 2nd Edition
How to Engage and Empower Your Students
Pernille Ripp

Passionate Readers:
The Art of Reaching and Engaging Every Child
Pernille Ripp

Engaging
Students
Using
Cooperative Learning

Second edition

John D. Strebe

Routledge
Taylor & Francis Group

NEW YORK AND LONDON

Second edition published 2018
by Routledge
711 Third Avenue, New York, NY 10017

and by Routledge
2 Park Square, Milton Park, Abingdon, Oxon, OX14 4RN

Routledge is an imprint of the Taylor & Francis Group, an informa business

© 2018 Taylor & Francis

First edition published by Eye On Education 2010

Library of Congress Cataloging-in-Publication Data
A catalog record for this book has been requested

ISBN: 978-1-138-63601-9 (hbk)
ISBN: 978-1-138-30263-1 (pbk)
ISBN: 978-1-315-17863-9 (ebk)

Typeset in Palatino
by Apex CoVantage, LLC

Visit the eResources: www.routledge.com/9781138302631

In Memory of Dr. David D. Strebe

Contents

About the Author

John Strebe taught secondary mathematics for 38 years in the Maryland public schools. For many years he has conducted workshops for teachers across the country, providing instruction on setting up a cooperative and engaging classroom.

John earned his B.S. in mathematics from the University of South Carolina and an M.A.T. degree from the Johns Hopkins University.

John and his wife Priscilla live in Bluffton, South Carolina. They have a son Jon, daughter-in-law Donna, daughter Sara, son-in-law Paul and 4 grand children, Luke, Ryan, Emma Kate and Benjamin.

For more information about John Strebe's workshops, visit http://JohnStrebe. blogspot.com or email him at JPJS@aol.com.

eResources

As you read this book, you'll notice the eResources icon next to the following tools. The icon indicates that these tools are available as free downloads on our website, www.routledge.com/9781138302631, so you can easily print and distribute them to your students.

Bonus: In addition to the six Pairs Check With a Switch samples in the book, extra examples are provided as eResources on our website.

Acknowledgements

The shaping of a person is a complex process with contributions provided by many people. All of the people listed in the bibliography have provided something for my professional growth as a teacher. Thanks to Robert Sickles for his many insights and special thanks to Jennifer Lee for her tireless work on the first edition of this manuscript and to Lauren Davis for her wise suggestions. A major component in my educational development was principal Dr. Edgar Markley, who treated me as a professional, arranged for the workshop where I first considered cooperative learning and gave me the freedom to fail as I attempted to implement these new strategies. Ed is a good friend and a tremendous leader in education. In addition, he taught me the importance of praise in the workplace by informally visiting my classroom and expressing his appreciation for what he had seen. Ellen Stine Miller conducted that first cooperative learning workshop and wonderfully communicated the fundamental concepts while personally challenging me to adopt them for my classroom. At Mt. Hebron High School, I had the benefit of being with capable, caring, passionate teachers and students who motivated me toward excellence. My students at Baltimore City College High School affirmed the worth of cooperative learning by their excellent classroom performance. Dr. Frank Lyman in his brilliance gave me the simple, but powerful principles of Think Time, Pair Time and Share Time. He also supplied much appreciated guidance as I created the manuscript for this book. For 30 years, Dr. Lynn Canady has encouraged me as I have conducted teacher workshops, recommending me as a trainer. He has shared much wisdom with me and, most important, has been a model of professionalism and integrity. Other than my father, he is the man I most admire in my experience. William Gerardi, a graduate college teacher, modeled the teaching of mathematics with energy and enthusiasm. Special thanks to teachers and educators in West Virginia who inspire me with their passion for excellence in teaching and for their words of encouragement. My parents, Roma and David Strebe, were career teachers, my mother in second grade and my father in college. Both loved children and were passionate about teaching. Dad was the best teacher I have ever experienced, teaching me the courses of topology and real analysis. My children, Jon, an excellent coach and teacher, and Sara, a talented orthopaedic surgeon, inspire me with their work ethic and character. My wife, Priscilla, the best woman ever made, is my rock and makes everything in my life wonderful and was my main editor of the manuscript. Finally, I thank God for calling me to teach and bringing all these wonderful people into my life.

Introduction

Writing this book is an exciting experience, especially as I consider who is probably reading it. Who reads a book on education when there are so many other attractive choices for spending our time? You are probably a person of passion, a person of three loves: a love for the subject you teach, a love for the students you inspire and a love for teaching. A teacher must have passion about the subject taught, especially if the students are going to love it as well. Personally, I love mathematics. I have a passion for learning about mathematical truth, studying the history of mathematics, re-reading mathematical truths first studied long ago and exploring new mathematical ideas. For me, the study of mathematics is better than sliced bread! What subject inspires you? Which subject do you love? Which set of ideas causes you joy? Your excitement will be contagious, enticing kids to invest themselves and to find joy in the subject you love.

The reader, no doubt, shares with me the love of children, the joy of being with young people who bring a certain naive freshness to our lives. They energize us with their enthusiasm about new ideas; they look at life in an unspoiled way, and they listen to our advice and life stories. Occasionally we can provide meaningful input and have a positive impact in their lives. Kids are a second passion teachers need to possess, thereby making each day of coming to work a new and rewarding adventure.

If you are reading this book, then you probably have a third passion, which is teaching your first passion, your subject, to your second, the students. Teaching mathematics to young folks, demonstrating mathematical truth to them for the first time, observing that excited look of discovery on their faces brought incomparable satisfaction to my heart as a mathematics teacher. There is a genuine adrenaline rush when the young person utters the words, "I got it!" A fellow teacher calls this the "math high." I am sure that teachers of other subjects experience this as well when chemical truths are discovered, skills of speaking and reading French are developed, the genius of Shakespeare is internalized, the events of a world war are relived and so many other new truths are enjoyed, perhaps for the first time. To be the one who introduces young minds to these great ideas is truly an amazing privilege.

Purpose

This book is about teaching, about helping students to engage in learning no matter what the subject being taught. Having passion is essential, but passion without effective teaching strategies can lead to extreme frustration. Passion should motivate the teacher to become an expert in the subject matter and to develop effective teaching skills.

Learning subject matter can require late nights of study, taking classes, reading, travel, seeking assistance from other teachers, hours on the Internet, all of which will require a patient perseverance. Loving the subject matter makes this determined study an enjoyable experience.

It is an undeniable observation that some people are born to teach, finding teaching as natural as a fish swimming in a lake. Others find teaching an awkward activity, experiencing many difficulties and frustrations. I believe that all of us need to discover better ways to teach, to learn new methods, to become better at doing what we love. If I cannot be a better teacher next year than I am this year, then this year should be my last year teaching.

I am presenting here some of the results of my 38-year search to become a better teacher. All of the strategies about which I am writing I borrowed from others or created myself and certainly adapted and used all of them for many years with all types of students.

For many years I have shared these ideas during teacher workshops and have been humbled and amazed as teachers from every discipline have used them with great success. I have visited classes where passionate teachers have used these ideas to teach culinary arts, English, history, auto mechanics, math, foreign language and many other subjects. Although my experience has been in secondary education, many teachers in elementary schools have adapted and used with great success the strategies described here. Recently, it has been my privilege to visit third and fourth grade classrooms taught by teachers who have incorporated these ideas. The students were focused, working together and having fun. After class, one of the fourth graders asked me if I had invented the cooperative team concepts. I told her that I had not, but I had trained her teacher to use them. The student's reply was, "Thanks. The teams are cool. They are fun!" I am convinced that engaging students in a collaborative way is an exciting and powerful way to learn.

Please understand that you are the expert in your classroom, and you are probably already doing amazing things with your students. As the expert, you will decide if anything included here can combine with what you already do to make you more effective and to enable your students to engage at a deeper level.

For me, student engagement includes kids learning to enjoy the subject that you teach and discussing that subject with other students as they seek to improve their understanding. I found that an effective way to do this was to structure the class into learning teams of two to five members and create a collaborative environment, something I first had to learn how to do. You get better at this the more you do it. I learned to effectively implement and control competition between the learning teams, providing incentive for student learning.

I will begin with my first day of classes and describe the first several days, after which I will write about various ideas, including doing worksheets cooperatively and lecturing interactively. I will describe ways to review material for a test as well as how to use quiz answers in a collaborative way. A major restructuring of a classroom based on the improvement of each student is fully presented. Various team builders are included as well as several ways to reengage students whose minds are wandering. A way of perceiving students is presented. The use of student enforcers is discussed. I have included a list of erroneous ideas for your thoughtful consideration and the questions most often asked at my workshops. Of special interest to me are the refreshingly honest responses of some of my students about learning in a cooperative setting.

In the movie *City Slickers,* Curly had that "one thing" which was the secret to living a meaningful life. My hope for you is that, by reading this book, you will find at least one thing that will prove valuable to you as you practice your passion of teaching. If that occurs, then you will have genuinely contributed to the substance of my life. I am grateful for this opportunity to share these thoughts.

The words "cooperative" and "collaborative" are used interchangeably. The goal is to create an *engaging* classroom experience.

A Warning

You and I do not teach the same students, nor do we have the same classroom furniture. We may not teach the same subject matter or even kids of the same age. Our personalities are different. If something written here seems good to you, please *adapt* it to you and your situation. Make it fit you and your students. Rename things; restructure them. To do this you will need to *create* and when you create, you are *renewed.* Becoming stagnant in your profession is no longer possible. Teacher burnout goes away. *Adapt, create and renew.*

The Block Schedule

Having students for extended periods of time provides opportunities to learn in a more focused setting. Often in a 45-minute class teachers and students are sprinting to a finish line. The extended block allows time to think, to reflect and to question ideas being considered in the class. Topics can be explored in depth and approached from a variety of directions. New topics can be presented, learned, applied and extended during one class period.

Developing relationships between student and student as well as between student and teacher becomes more essential and more possible in a block schedule. The additional time makes it possible and essential to use activities which deepen relationships. As students work together, learning is enhanced.

In the extended block the learning environment of a classroom stands out; a negative atmosphere becomes unbearable, creating a group of clock watchers and moaners, but a positive one benefits from the increased amount of continuous time together participating in profitable and engaging activities with a "family" of learners. The material in this book may help teachers create a more desirable learning community as they make advantageous use of a block schedule.

In every learning situation some students will wander mentally, sometimes after only a few minutes of a lecture or other learning activity. Most students seem to lose that sharp learning readiness at some point in a lesson. If the teacher does not do something to bring the kids back, a loss of learning opportunities results. Suppose a majority of the students are not focused after 20 minutes. In a 45-minute class, 25 minutes of learning are compromised; in a 90-minute class, reduced learning occurs for 70 minutes. In a classroom of 30 students, 2100 minutes of valuable learning is lost. The skilled teacher becomes adept at recognizing when this happens or is about to occur and introduces a change to the environment that causes students to reengage. I call these changes "**educational interrupters**." These interrupters include determining how and when materials are distributed, structuring how material is reviewed, changing who is talking and who is listening, starting a new activity and changing where the students are sitting. This refresh of the learning set is always important, but especially so in the block.

The ideas and strategies written about here were used by me for 26 of the 38 years I taught, the last 14 in three different block schedules. I hope that using them brings you as much joy as I have experienced.

Some Possible Reader Responses

"You just do not know my kids. This will not work with them. You probably only taught the gifted and talented classes." I do not know your kids, but I do know kids and they would rather cooperate, engage and enjoy learning than be constantly talked at or controlled or bored. Cooperative learning was enjoyed by my students in a suburban school as well as kids I taught in the inner city. Most years I was privileged to teach at least two classes of Introduction to Algebra composed of severely challenged students, most of whom were learning disabled, as well as several classes like Algebra 2 GT, Pre-Calculus or Advanced Placement Calculus. I am convinced that cooperative learning provides an environment for maximum learning independent of course level or a student's ability. Using cooperative learning will not guarantee success, but it does provide additional tools with which to address student needs.

Chapter 1

The First Day

The First Day

The first day of school is filled with anticipation and excitement for every passionate teacher. Several days prior to meeting my students I prepare for their arrival by arranging the desks into pairs or groups of four and five. (*see* A Pairs Class *and* A Four's Class *on page 4.*) Notice the "fan" arrangement of the desks which ensures that no student has to turn more than 90 degrees to see the front of the class. Also notice that groups of four are arranged so that no student has to look through the head of a teammate but can see the teacher without obstruction. Furniture arrangement is a key factor in establishing effective cooperation. Hanging from the ceiling above the center of each group is a piece of colorful yarn with a laminated number attached, marking the location of each group. I use the numbers 2 through 10. When I was a "floater," pushing a cart around the halls, teaching in several rooms, I used gummed labels stuck to the dividers between the ceiling tiles to mark these locations. Identifying group locations is especially helpful when an ambitious custodian cleans the room but leaves the desks against the walls. A simple instruction from me, "Kids, arrange your groups under the numbers" resulted in the room being ready for the day. Students were also taught, depending on the coming activity, to convert the room to a "team" structure or a "pairs" arrangement. This allowed me to conserve my energy and begin to communicate to the students that this was not "my" room, but it was "our" room. Our journey into the collaborative classroom had begun. Telling the present class that the previous class had arranged the desks in 20 seconds adds a spirit of competition and usually the task was performed in less time by subsequent classes.

As each student arrives at the room, a firm handshake and greeting is given. "My name is Mr. Strebe, what is your name? Are you sure you are in my Algebra 2 class? Great to meet you! Sit wherever you wish." For me, this is a very emotional time. As I would look into the eyes of each student, I am impressed with the fact that the two of us would have many opportunities to make an impression on each other during the year. Neither of us would ever again be the same because we have spent the year together, learning from each other, experiencing life together, growing through difficult times and rejoicing in wonderful successes. How blessed I am to be called to teach!

A Pairs Class

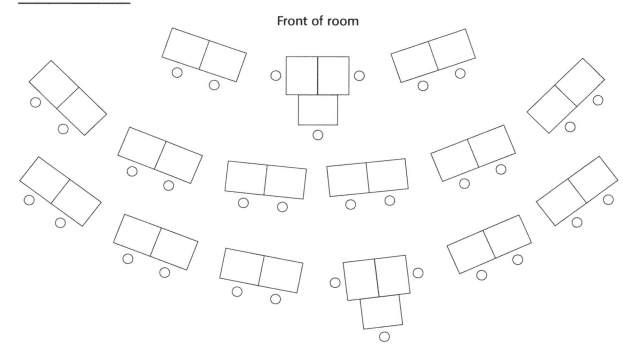

Front of room

A Four's Class

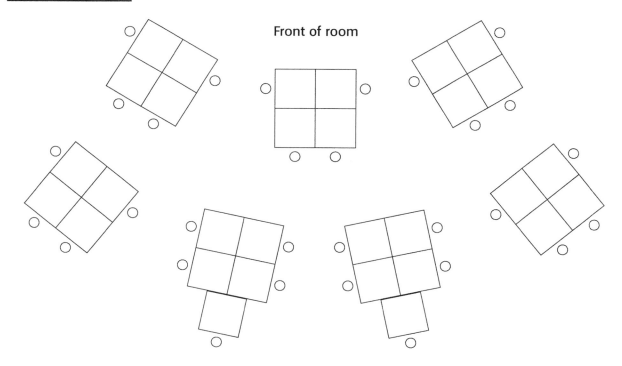

Front of room

On that first day most of the students choose to sit near students with whom they are familiar, often with good friends. I desire to put them into teams for the first day where the comfort level is not so high. Suppose there are 24 people in the class. Twenty-four divided by 4 is 6. I take from a full deck those cards numbered from 2 through 7 from each suit and distribute them to each group in numerical order by suit. If this is done properly, each person in a group will have a different number than the others.

Nonverbal Cues

I then develop a **nonverbal cue** that we will use all year. When my arm is raised, we know it is a sign for silence and that a question requiring a chorus response is coming. They should look into my eyes in anticipation. I ask them to look at the color of the card—either red or black. On the count of 3, my arm will be lowered and the class choruses the color on each card, saying "red" or "black." I respond, "Way to go! This is a capable group of people." My arm is raised again and the kids look into my eyes and listen as I instruct, "Look at the number on your card. Ask a neighbor if you are unsure—after all, it has been a long summer." Each student identifies the number on the card and on the count of 3, my arm is lowered and the class choruses each number. *Nonverbal cues are powerful tools.* This one is used every day in every class during the year.

Now the students are instructed to repeat the words, "Different color. Different number. Different table." These words are repeated twice more. The students are then instructed to pair up with someone having a card of a different number with a different color who is sitting in a different group. If the number of students in the class is an odd number, then some lucky student will pair up with the teacher.

Students are encouraged to think about a cool activity they had enjoyed that summer. It could be a trip taken, a game attended or played or something ordinary like sleeping late. They are encouraged to think and not speak. "Make this your secret." On cue the students with the larger card number in each pair call out in chorus, "I have the larger number." The student with the larger number then shares the cool activity from the summer with the student who has the lowest number. Then the student with the lowest number shares with the person possessing the highest number.

At this time everyone learns how to touch another person in an acceptable manner—remember, this could be a secondary setting. We give each other a" high five" or we give each other a "pound" or we shake hands. Each pair touches each other in one of these ways and expresses verbal thanks for the shared secret. Developing **the habit of saying thanks** to each other helps create a "family" climate in the classroom, a place where each person belongs and where learning can occur at an optimum level. *Touching each other helps to break through personal barriers* each of us brings to a classroom.

The next activity involves **movement with a purpose** as each student is instructed to find the other students having the same numbered card and create a huddle with them, memorizing the day and month of birth of each one in this new group. So, all the "2's" are memorizing the birth facts as are all the "3's", the "4's" and so on. After a short time, the students sit in the numbered location (hanging from the ceiling) that matches the number on the card. The students move all their belongings to this new group. They are encouraged to review the birthdates in each team. For this first day only, good friends will probably not be together. If some of the students are known by the teacher, the handing out of the cards can be orchestrated so that certain students are not together while others have been purposely given the same number. One or two volunteers from the class recite the birth dates of each member of the group after which the class claps for this feat of memory. *Clapping for each other helps with class climate.* I ask the student if that could have been accomplished without the assistance and help of the other three students and, of course, the answer is "no." I then make that student a promise that if, in the same way, the members of the group are considered as resources during the study of mathematics, learning math will take less time; the math concepts will be remembered longer and learning math will be much more fun.

To illustrate that, we then learn mathematics for the next 15 minutes or so. The kids are enthusiastic, engaged, locked in and ready to learn. After this first segment of learning some students are beginning to drift away mentally and need to be brought back in. It is the first day of school after a long summer away from classes. How can these students be reengaged? The main office has supplied the necessary equipment for this.

Fortunately, it is the first day of school and we tend to welcome our young people to their new community by drowning them in paper, handing out lunch information sheets, insurance forms, bus tickets, the school code of discipline, Internet forms, locker assignments and anything else which will fit on an 8.5 by 11 inch piece of paper. Handing out these materials allows students to take a necessary break. I distribute papers to the students by having one person from each team come to pick up enough forms for the entire team. Perhaps I will ask the student from each team with the earliest birth date in the year, or the person wearing the most blue today, or the person with the shortest or longest hair to come pick up the various documents. Forms that need to be collected are brought to me by the person in the team who might have been at McDonald's most recently. When students get up out of their seats to accomplish an educational purpose, the learning environment is refreshed, and the teacher is spared the experience of performing the athletic miracle of walking around the room and not falling flat after catching a foot in a book bag strap. When one or more of the forms have been distributed, we get to do it again—we learn in a collaborative setting and have much fun doing it.

Educational Interrupters

After each 15-minute segment, an **educational interrupter** is used to reengage all students. On the first day, these interrupters have been generously supplied by the administration requiring teachers to distribute many papers. The class continues in this fashion, fulfilling all the requirements of the main office and experiencing the joy, beauty and thrill of mathematics. Do not waste the value of this interrupter by handing out the office's papers at the beginning of the class. Wait until the students' attention begins to wane. Depending on the class, interrupters may be necessary after as little as 7 minutes or not until 20 minutes have passed. You are the expert and will determine the correct time to bring the kids back. Toward the end of our class, the "person wearing the most blue" picks up textbooks and information cards for the entire group. The person with the latest birth date in each team could bring the teacher one completed textbook information card for each person. Homework is assigned—yes, homework is given on the first day of school. After all, I love math and I love kids so I will not keep these two loves apart for another night. One or more students will remark about having homework on the first day of school and I ask them if they know why I give them homework. "It is because I love you! If I ever forget to give you homework, please question my care for you." Sure enough, one day I purposely hold back the assignment and Larry asks whether or not I still love them. I feign shock, give the homework, assure them of my love and ask them to thank Larry who is now in deep trouble with the class. The first night's homework is a math assignment *and* the task of reading and studying my syllabus. In addition, the students are to bring the syllabus to the next class.

Notice that on the first day I used no time in class to present my class rules. Students have been engaged in learning the subject matter, participated in small team competitions and actively distributed many documents. Every minute has been filled with activity, and there has been no down time.

The last thing the kids do is print their first and last names on one side of a color-coded 3 by 5 card (a different color for each class period). An announcement is made that a quiz on the syllabus— yes, a *real* quiz, one that will count and be recorded in the grade book—will be given during the next class.

As the kids leave I meet them at the door, shake hands, look each student in the eye and tell them a hearty and sincere "Thanks for being here." Our adventure together has begun, and I am looking forward to the next class, but only after an evening of refreshment and contemplation.

The first day of school in this math class has been activity filled, productive and fun. This was not always the case in my career and the change must be credited to my son when he was an eighth-grader. Jon came home after his first day and I expected him to have a more joyful attitude than the one he had. After all it *was* the first day of school! You get to see your friends, brag about your summer and even be reunited with an occasional cool teacher. Instead, his response was, "Dad, I am back in jail again!" I wondered how that could be true. He said, "Well, Dad, stay with me here. First period was English and do you know what we did? Heard the rules. Second period was math and more rules. Then came social studies and the teacher dictated the rules." The story was the same for each of the 7 periods. Jon *was* correct. He *was* back in jail again. I had never looked at the first day of school through the eyes of a student. What Jon described was not a good phenomenon. I determined that I would never again have a first-day experience that would be dull and boring and rules filled. Up until that moment I had not appreciated the students' total first-day experience. I had not looked at them beyond the time I had them in my class. Often students have said to me at the end of my "new" first day that this class was the most fun they had all day—and they were learning mathematics besides! Truly, kids can teach us much if we listen.

On the evening of the first day of school I was usually exhausted and fatigued—it had been a long summer for me too. Those nonstudent days in August had allowed me to get my room ready, to prepare lesson plans and renew with staff, but nothing gets you ready for that first day filled with interactions and challenges. It was a good tired because I was expending much energy doing something I loved—teaching kids. After a wonderful meal and conversation with the best woman God ever created, my dear wife, it was time to prepare for the next day. I lay out the blue name cards from period 1 on my dining room table, one of my most valuable educational tools. I arrange the cards into *pairs*, reflecting on the students I observed on the first day, thinking about their personalities, how they interacted with other students, what needs and strengths were displayed. The purpose is to put each student with a partner or partners with whom they will work well, based on the very superficial information from my memory and from notes I took during the first class. If the number of students in the class is an odd number, one trio will be needed. This process is repeated for each class using the color-coded cards, matching pairs of students by observed strengths and needs. If I am on an alternating day schedule, I have two days to accomplish this task.

For me, this is a very familiar and comfortable way to manage the first day. Some may find it cumbersome, especially the first time implemented. It may be advisable to use this student-matching process in just a few classes, perhaps only one class, until the necessary skills are achieved. Creating a collaborative classroom can be started at most any time during the school year. The teacher, who is the expert in the classroom, should make these decisions and will eventually become proficient.

Chapter 2

First Weeks

Pairs Rehearsal

The next day in each class I set up the room with pairs of students (*see* A Pairs Class, on page 4) and lay the name cards on the desktops, greeting the students at the door with a handshake and "name reminder" exchange. "Mr. Strebe, where do we sit?" The instruction is given to find your card and sit there with your partner for today. For some classes, having a written record of pairings might be a good idea; funny how some of those cards have legs. The first activity is to use the syllabus and do **Pairs Rehearsal.**

Collaborative Pairs

PAIRS REHEARSAL

Do your students ever need to refresh their minds just before a quiz? Do your students ever need to review material in preparation for a lesson that requires previous knowledge? Would you like *all* students to participate in building their skills? Would you like even the quietest student to share with another person? Would you like the loud, dominant student to let others share truth also?

Pairs Rehearsal may be for you. Divide the class into pairs. One trio may be required or the teacher may be a partner as well. One player could be designated "purple" and the other "orange." The teacher should supply content to be discussed or students may use notes from a previous class. A list of questions or a review sheet containing important facts would suffice. Students could be asked to take out their class notes and/or an information sheet about a particular topic. A book could serve as the chief resource. Students may want to decide which resources would be helpful during this activity.

The pairs face each other and the teacher supplies a time limit for the activity. The "orange" person tells the "purple" person a fact from the content area using any appropriate resource. The "purple" person then tells the "orange" person a different fact. The two share different facts in an alternating fashion until the time has expired. If the facts are exhausted, already shared facts can be shared again. Instead of sharing a fact, students can ask each other questions from a prepared sheet or from a set of questions that they might have generated in a previous activity or homework assignment. Discussion of the questions deepens the learning. Each student is accountable to a partner.

In each sharing the listener must think carefully and correct any error stated by the partner. The speaker attempts to share vital facts, writing explanations where needed.

If a trio of students is necessary, a third color, perhaps "red," is assigned and the process follows a sequence like "orange," "purple" and "red".

The teacher should be roaming the room, listening to the sharing of the pairs. If a pair has trouble getting started, the teacher could join them and "prime the pump" of the sharing process, being careful to offer specific praise for effective interaction.

The teacher may find it helpful to form specific pairs of students depending on observed strengths and needs of the kids. This re-pairing can be just for this present activity. In some classes, random pairing works well.

Pairs Rehearsal can be used for several minutes just prior to a test to get students in the right mind set to produce excellence. It could be used to establish a solid knowledge base required to learn additional concepts. For example, suppose we had studied inverse functions during our previous class on Thursday, an "A" day of our alternating schedule. On Monday, school was cancelled due to excessive snowfall. The class was not scheduled to meet on Wednesday because an assembly would be held. During our next class on Friday we needed to study logarithms, but it had been over a week since we had been together to discuss inverse functions, a concept necessary for the understanding of logarithms. This is a good time to do **Pairs Rehearsal** recalling inverse functions. During this time it is the students who are saying the facts aloud to each other and not just the teacher doing the talking. After all, it is the students who need to be interacting about these facts and not the teacher who has already mastered the facts.

On the second day of school, after students have reviewed the syllabus using **Pairs Rehearsal,** allowing a time for asking the teacher questions prepares them further for the quiz on the syllabus. The desks are moved apart and a 20-question quiz on the syllabus is given to the students. They are allowed to keep the syllabus on their desks and refer to it for facts and information. Have some extra copies nearby because some kids will not have them secured in their notebooks. The true goal for today is that each student cooperates and learns the class policies. Once the students are finished, they are asked if they would like to compare their answers with another student and make any changes they wish. Classes have always responded to this in a positive way—remember, the grade goes into the grade book. The desks are put back into their pairs and discussion ensues. I roam the class encouraging good defense of ideas. This experience teaches kids the value of other students' thoughts and perspectives. Consensus is not the goal. Interaction about the subject matter at hand is the goal. Changing of recorded answers is optional. At an appropriate time, the quizzes are collected and put away to be graded later. My experience has been that the students know and understand the syllabus much better than when I used to drone my way through it on the first day of school. They have also experienced some of the skills and the value of collaboration. Most of the grades are 90% or better.

Now we get to do math in a collaborative setting, remembering to use educational interrupters at given intervals of time in order to bring every person into the learning. We end class with a *purposeful* homework assignment, pairs thanking each other for the help given and received. I find it is also helpful to have the pairs touch each other in the learned approved ways as thanks are expressed.

That night I take the name cards for each class and arrange them into purposefully chosen trios, again considering the needs, strengths and weaknesses of the students to match them well. Incidentally, groups of 3 are especially appropriate in classes where decisions are made, controversial topics discussed or opinions expressed. Having a tie-breaker in each group is helpful. The matches are much better with the additional day of observation and the increased information I have gathered.

The third class day begins with a handshake, and the students finding their cards and new groups. The next day they are in groups of 4, and the next day in groups of 2 and so on until I feel confident about knowing who my students are both academically and personally. Often a comment is made like, "Mr. Strebe, we never know where we are sitting in here!" I usually point out how exciting that is and observe that it is not like church, where although seats are not assigned, people tend to sit in the same location week after week.

I remember once when doing a workshop in Williamsburg, Virginia, my wife and I attended the early service on Palm Sunday at Bruton Parish Church. We arrived well before the service began and were doing some quiet meditation when I became aware of two elderly people staring at us intensely. Performing a quick inventory of my behavior I suddenly realized that our offense was that we were sitting in "their" seats. Although our love for math borders on the sacred, the class is not church, and we do change our seats frequently at the beginning of the year. This flexibility has been of great benefit for the students and teacher alike.

Warnings

After 26 years of teaching collaboratively and 24 years of conducting collaborative workshops, I have concluded that three major errors are responsible for less than satisfactory results in the interactive classroom.

♦ Team size was inappropriate for the class.

♦ Team membership was not carefully, thoughtfully and purposefully decided.

♦ Team building was not adequately done.

Final Teams

After deciding to create a collaborative environment, the next decision should be about the **size** of teams in each class. Generally, where class management is more of a challenge the initial groups should be pairs because they are easier to administer. Teams of 4 are appropriate for classes where management is less of a factor. Teams of 3 are beneficial for classrooms where discussions will provoke opinions to be expressed because a third person can be utilized to break ties when determining team conclusions. Each teacher will need to decide the appropriate size of the teams for each class. Forming teams that are too large can result in excessive off-task behavior. Teams that are too small can limit the perspectives shared and heard during a time of discussion.

After observing a class for about 6 to 10 days, sometimes longer or shorter, I feel somewhat confident about my knowledge of the students. It is time to form the teams according to their *personal characteristics.* In a 4's class, teams of 5 exist with the fifth person being a student with an attendance problem. When the habitually absent student is gone, the team still has 4 people, which helps interaction. These 4 people are invaluable in helping the absentee student upon returning to school. Similarly, in a 2's class, groups of 3 will be completed by the kid who is frequently absent from school.

An attempt is made to have a *mix of academic strengths on each team and to have academic parity in the teams;* however, *personal traits* dominate the team selection process. For example, a student newly arrived from Korea should have, if possible, a bilingual team member or at least a team member who is an effective communicator. The autistic student may benefit from a caring, hands-off person. A quiet, insecure student needs a sensitive team member, someone who does not pose a threat. A young man who acts out demonstrably will benefit by being placed with the "right" three girls. His behavior is muted or mollified, thus giving benefit to the class as well. If he were to be placed with another male, a struggle for "pecking order in the yard" can occur. Many other considerations prevail and you, the expert, will do an adequate job initially and a great job eventually in making these choices. Investing your time in the making of final placements will give you positive returns many times over. Every student has strengths and needs. Take care to match a student with the **strength** to help meet another student with a specific **need.** Resist the temptation to rush through the team selection process.

One Way to Form a Power-Balanced Team

When competition points are based upon raw scores, establishing teams that have similar scoring power may be advisable.

Suppose a class has 24 students, requiring 6 teams to be formed. Six students can be labeled with an H, meaning high achiever *with respect to the students in this class.* The designation with an H refers to the performance of the student in this class up to the present. The names are written on a paper like this:

Tom(H)   Molly(H)   Suzie(H)   Lavonda(H)   Willie(H)   Ben(H)

Next a designation of L could be assigned to 6 students indicating that the performance in this class has been not good and write the names like this:

Tom(H)   Molly(H)   Suzie(H)   Lavonda(H)   Willie(H)   Ben(H)

Sam(L)   Nancy(L)   John(H)   Sherry(L)   Pam(L)   Eloise(L)

The remainder of the students are labeled with an A, indicating that their performance in this class so far has not been poor nor has it been outstanding.

The possible teams now are written as follows:

Tom(H)	Molly(H)	Suzie(H)	Lavonda(H)	Willie(H)	Ben(H)
James(A)	Paul(A)	Rachel(A)	Rebecca(A)	Sandy(A)	Sheila(A)
Tony(A)	Carla(A	Melanie(A)	Chan(A)	Rhonda(A)	Lanny(A)
Sam(L)	Nancy(L)	John(L)	Sherry(L)	Pam(L)	Eloise(L)

Keep in mind the **strengths** and **needs** of each student as each is placed on a team.

Make obvious changes, attempting to switch an A with an A, an H for an H and an L with an L. This will result in one of the first trial teams. Try the arrangement in class and then reflect on who worked well together. Make changes and observe the outcomes in the next class. Continue this process until the arrangement results in a workable classroom.

Suppose there are two students who have demonstrated a pattern of absence from school. Each of those students should be placed on a team with 5 members. Team sizes might be 5, 5, 4, 4, 3, and 3. In a pairs class two groups of 3 would be needed.

NOTE: Balancing teams by power is not vital for Carolina Teams since the team performance is based on *improvement* and not raw scores. The strengths and the needs of the students are the primary factors in successful team formation (SEE CHAPTER 9).

On the first day that "final" teams are used, seat the kids as usual using the cards. Make final observations during that class and determine if good decisions have been made. Refrain from telling the students that these are the final teams until a time near the close of the class; this will allow you to fix any errors made in team formation before the next class. Once you are comfortable, the students can be told to sit in these seats tomorrow. Of course, you will have written down the names of students in each team, just in case a student "forgets" which is his team.

These teams will stay together about 8 to 10 weeks. If you are in a 4 by 4 block, you may wish to shorten the number of weeks the kids are in these teams. You will know when it is time to change teams or even change the number of people in the teams, for example, going from a 4's class to a 2's class. A warning—sometimes if this is working well, you may give in to the temptation to leave the teams together longer, just because of the benefits and the fact that it is easier not to disturb the arrangement. At some point, new teams need to be formed, providing students with the experience of working with kids who are not necessarily as good a match for them as those in the original group. Our students will live and work in a social climate and need the opportunity to improve and test out new interactive skills, especially with students different from themselves, even those with whom they would not choose to sit in the school cafeteria.

Chapter 3

Team Building/ Class Building

Team Building/Class Building

In addition to careful team selection, a vital step in the creation of productive teams is solid *team building*. One of the most powerful team builders I use is the **Things In Common** sheet, three versions of which are included here. A leader in each team is selected, perhaps the "best dancer," and each is given a TIC sheet with the instructions to return to the team and find 10 things on which they could agree, not our favorite things or our least favorite things, but something all 4 of us like or all 4 of us dislike. For example, if all members of the group like pizza, then pizza could be the food entry for things we all like. If 3 of the 4 people do not like liver, but one person likes liver, then liver can not be the entry for food we dislike. The items entered must receive a unanimous vote of the team. The team leaders are given about 3 minutes to complete the task.

The **Things In Common** activity can be powerfully used with any size group, including pairs of students.

The teacher should roam the room helping slow-starting teams to begin, perhaps even pulling up a chair and helping a team to get its first entry. Encourage slow-working teams to skip around when stuck on a particular topic. After a period of time announce the end of the activity. Do not make completion of the activity controversial. Statements like, "You have one minute to finish. Hurry up!" are not appropriate here. The true goal was *not* to complete the activity, but *for the team members to talk with each other.* Perhaps the team that did not finish talked the most because they had trouble arriving at agreement. The teams are developing their team communication skills using familiar things, and later they will use these same skills to discuss profound academic topics. The kids are also discovering that although we are all different, we have many things in common and throughout the year we will discover that we all rejoice about good things, hurt when bad things happen, become frustrated when we fail and celebrate when we succeed. While celebrating our diversity, we can gain strength and comfort when we realize all the things we have in common. In the collaborative classroom we can develop and exercise skills that will allow us to affect in positive ways our environment now and in the future. Realizing all the things we share can help us to help each other.

THINGS IN COMMON

Form A

WE ALL WE ALL WE ALL WE ALL WE ALL WE ALL WE ALL WE ALL WE ALL WE ALL

	LIKE	DISLIKE
Food		
Place To Go		
Activity		
Movie Or TV Show		
Anything You Choose (no category)		

Team Name _____

Engaging Students Using Cooperative Learning, John Strebe © Taylor & Francis

THINGS IN COMMON

Form B

WE ALL WE ALL WE ALL WE ALL WE ALL WE ALL WE ALL WE ALL WE ALL WE ALL

LIKE _____ DISLIKE _____

Season Of The Year

Fast Food

Place To Shop

Car

Anything You Want

_____

Team Name _____

THINGS IN COMMON

Form C

WE ALL WE ALL WE ALL WE ALL WE ALL WE ALL WE ALL WE ALL WE ALL WE ALL

	LIKE	DISLIKE
Music Or Song Or Singer		
Sport		
Shoes		
Day Of The Week		
Anything You Choose		

Team Name _____

Reflection on Collaboration

If I should reach the age of 80 and still possess the ability to reflect on my life, I will feel I have lived a good life if my students have learned to think logically, have learned to do mathematical analysis and even sing the quadratic formula. If, however, that is all they have learned from me, then I will feel I have wasted a wonderful opportunity to teach them empathy, patience, how to show love and mercy, how to comfort, how to respect others, in essence how to be thoughtful, caring human beings. If they have learned and practiced these things in my math class, then I will feel I have lived a substantial life. What an opportunity we teachers have to affect the lives of young people in positive ways! It has been my experience that as students improve their interpersonal skills in a collaborative classroom, their academic accomplishment is improved as well. It does not have to be a choice between the teaching of academics *or* the teaching of values, rather, teaching one enhances the other. Reorganizing my classroom from rows of individuals to cooperating teams has increased the opportunities for growth in both of these areas.

Sometimes Kids Don't Listen

Many years ago I asked for the person from each team with the longest hair to meet me for instructions. Although there were 8 teams, only 4 people met me at the desired location. Half the teams had not done what I asked. I learned to get a **visual response** before asking them to meet me. After asking them to find the person with the longest hair I ask each of these people to raise a hand in the air. Once I see a hand for each team, then I ask them to get up and meet me. The result is that 8 out of 8 people come to the desired location. It is a simple thing, but visual response works!

Celebration

My son is a head varsity girls' basketball coach and a good one. For a time I had the privilege of being his assistant, and I remember when our team was playing a team our school had never beaten. The crowd was noisy, the mascot jumping and the air charged with electricity—a great memorable environment. When the clock read 0:00 our team had scored more points than the competition and I watched as our parents, students and other fans celebrated the team victory. We never taught them when or how to celebrate, they just knew.

I often have the opportunity to walk the hallways of schools and as I pass doorway after doorway of academic classes, I rarely witness celebration. It is my belief that learning should be the hardest work that is ever done and yet at the same time, the most fun. We should celebrate accomplishment, both team and class success. Often I will teach celebration by showing the first team finished with the TIC sheet one way to celebrate. While the rest of the class is continuing the activity, I show them the "**Strebe High 1.**" I join them and we touch index fingers of our right hands in the middle of the group, making an arc as we raise them in the air. Simultaneously, we reach straight out with our left arms, fists clenched, and pull the left hand back while whispering, "yesssss."

Once the TIC activity is completed, the demonstration team shows the class this way to celebrate and all teams practice. Kids will want to know when it is appropriate to celebrate. Any time a team finishes an activity or accomplishes something are the times to celebrate. One Monday the class was doing the first activity and a team did the "High 1" much sooner than expected. I asked them what that was about and one person recounted how Billy, a member of their team, had won a motocross race over the weekend. They got it!

Celebrate! This experience also revealed that the classroom was authentic, that a certain amount of socialization could profitably accompany academic work. There simply needs to be a balance between the two. Sometimes teams will create their own unique manner of celebration like the swimming fish, the home run hitters or the wigglers with appropriate pantomimes. I encourage teams to celebrate all team accomplishment. Teaching a mode of celebration and creating an expectancy for celebration builds team spirit as well as making the class experience joy and fulfillment.

The TIC sheets can be taken to the teacher by the "best singer" in each group—*do not forget to get a visual response* by each "best singer" first. The sheets could be put away until the next class when at an appropriate time—that time is often after about 15 minutes—I take out the stack of papers, shuffle them and make up a story using one of the sheets. "Here is a team that could go out to dinner together and they would have pizza without liver. They would eat the pizza without liver at the beach and stay away from all doctors. They love to go shopping, but they would hire other people to clean their bathrooms. They love to watch Superman but when reality shows come on they go back to the beach to eat more pizza without liver. When they play music they love to listen to country, and they hope the NY Yankees lose."

Now the teams confer and one team guesses the identity of the team whose sheet I used to create the story. A tangible reward, like a lollipop or a special pencil, can be given to the guessing team if they are correct, or the reward is given to the team that authored the sheet if the guess is incorrect. The activity is an exercise in **class building**. Often I will hear, "Mr. Strebe, can you read another story?" I respond that it is a good idea and we will. The next story will be done as an interrupter when students need to be reengaged. Over several days team stories will continue to be read to the class until each team's story has been read. This activity helps to create team identity and pride, and by using it, the class is pulled together as well.

Team Names

The sheets are put away and the class continues. During a subsequent class each team picks up their Things In Common sheet and the person wearing the most blue reads all their likes and dislikes to the team using their team voice, not their class voice. The teams are now encouraged to use the TIC sheet to create a team name, a name that reflects their likes and/or dislikes. The team name should not be degrading, no worse than neutral, hopefully uplifting and a name deserving of the pride of all members of the team. It is helpful to show them team names from past teams, like PIZZA LIVERS, BEACH SPROUTS, 3 BRUNETTES AND A BLONDE, THE ALGEBRA GUESSERS or THE FAB 4. One of my favorite names came from a group composed of 4 girls, 2 Caucasians and 2 African Americans. The girls were very excited about showing me this name and called me over to see it—they were called VANILLA COKE. How creative is that?! It is my role as teacher to make this name, this special group identity, be the focus of their activities, the incentive to work hard, the reason they all do homework and the object for performing well on quizzes. I want to hear students making statements such as, "We want our team to win."

Sometimes a team will struggle to create a team name. This should not be a controversial process. The teacher can help by looking at the TIC sheet and making a creative, amusing suggestion. The teacher might suggest the name SWIMMING RADISHES and indicate that it will be their name if the team does not come up with another name in two or three days. One of two responses is usually made by the team. One person might say something like, "Don't worry, we'll definitely have a name by then," indicating the team does not want that silly name. On the other hand, the response could be, "We like that name. We are the Swimming Radishes." Make the process enjoyable.

Team Names for Grades K, 1 and Some 2

A simple and sure procedure for creating team names in the primary grades can be done using the Think, Team, Share strategy. Ask each person in Think Mode to think about a color for their team. During Team Mode the team decides on one Team Color. The process is repeated with the goal to select a Team Animal. The team names have been generated—Pink Panthers, Gold Tigers, Blue Dogs, Green Cats, etc. The teacher records the team names and later creates the name label to be posted in the classroom.

At this time or at a later class, each team is given a rectangular piece of paper and magic markers to create their team name, usually with artwork. I cut pieces of copy paper in half and give each team a piece of paper about 5 by 8 inch size. Kids are allowed to take the paper home, and they are given several days to complete the task, but the amount of class time used for this activity should be held to a minimum. Team names are placed on a scoreboard, often a laminated poster board with tape rollbacks to affix the names. Next to each name are several small squares of plain paper. These small squares will be used to record the points the team earns doing various activities.

Soft competition will be used to encourage teams to work hard and to perform well. If there are 6 or more teams, it is helpful to have 2 divisions so that on championship day there can be at least two winning teams. Competitions run for about 5 or 6 school days, 2 weeks for an alternating schedule or about 1 week if the schedule is a 4 by 4 block. After an appropriate period of time, champions are determined and rewarded, and the points are taken down so a new competition can begin. The teams stay the same, but you can place teams in new divisions to guarantee at least one new winner the next time. Changing the teams within the divisions is best done when the students are gone for the day.

For the teacher who is a "floater" or a "cart pusher," wall space is sometimes minimal, depending on the room. The solution can be to purchase from a home improvement supply store white shower board, which comes in 4 by 8 foot pieces and have it cut into thirds. Team names and points squares can be taped easily to the board. Then, the boards can be conveniently stored behind file cabinets until the next class when they can be placed on chalk trays for display.

Building Caring Relationships

Quality caring relationships between teachers and students can have a profound effect on the learning in the classroom. I think about this and try to emphasize relationship from the first time I meet each student. On the first day of school I like to have all my class preparations completed prior to the start of class so that I can meet each student at the door with a firm handshake and an enthusiastic welcome. This is time I like to spend getting to know my kids and letting them start getting to know me. Sharing information about summer activities, favorite sports teams, other classes taught and taken, extra curricular interests, common acquaintances and other things helps to break down that adversarial wall that seems to naturally exist between teachers and students. Developing effective communication will reap many rewards during the year.

Good relationships are built upon the knowledge we have of each other. Near the beginning of the year I share with the kids my goals for the year, that each of them **become a scholar** in all they do, that each of them **grow in character** and that every student **improve their math skills**. Each student is given a copy of the class goals and using Think/Pair/Square/Share (explained in a later chapter) the students ask questions, any question, about the goals. Using Circle of Knowledge (also explained later) allows each team to ask at least one question. The discussion allows me to communicate with the students in depth about the class and gives us a good beginning to our relationship, especially as I use personal experiences and stories from my life to explain some of the goals.

The goals are three-hole-punched and placed in each student's notebook for future reference. Make a poster of the goals for quick reference. One positive feature about being a "floater" is having a moving billboard, your cart, with the goals taped to it.

Several days later it is my turn to find out about my students. Each student is given a piece of paper and asked to put his or her name at the top. They are asked to determine their ages in 5 years and in 15 years. On the paper the following is typed with appropriate space to respond. They are:

Write your age 5 years from now_____.
What do you hope to be doing in 5 years?

Write your age in 15 years_____.
What do you hope to have accomplished and be doing in 15 years?

When you leave this class in June, what do you hope to have learned?

Prior to writing it is a good idea to suggest that the students write only things that they are willing to share with others.

When the students have finished writing, pairs of students exchange papers, read and ask each other questions about what they read. At the end of the sharing, they shake hands and say thanks. Two new pairs in the group repeat the process and then the last pair exchange and talk. The last pair should change their seating so they are sitting next to or across from each other, but not diagonally from each other. Then, I have the person wearing the most blue bring me all the papers from their team. This information is a very important part in my getting to know my students. Throughout the course I am able to address my students' goals for their lives and I am able to make what we learn personal for the kids. It is very instructive for the students to have learned about the goals of other students as well.

The students know what drives me and I know a bit about their lives. Now we are able to have a more profitable year of growth together. Having this information gives me sensitivity to programs which would be of special interest to my students. I can use examples which would relate to some of their goals. I can introduce the kids to people who share those same goals, fellow students and adults already established in related professions.

SAMPLE CLASS GOALS

BECOME A SCHOLAR

learn to love to learn
do your homework for understanding, not to just get it done
make excellence your goal
learn to focus
be on time
be present
fulfill all your academic responsibilities
never give up
replace whining with thanksgiving
use all your resources

DEVELOP YOUR CHARACTER

care about others
encourage and praise others
help others to do what is right
develop personal toughness with a gentle spirit
embrace justice, not might
walk in your integrity
practice honesty
reject mediocrity in all forms
practice empathy
truth it
learn to cope, not to blame

IMPROVE YOUR MATH SKILLS

generate and recognize mathematical truth
make a mathematically sound defense of conclusions
master all skills necessary for success in the next math course
enjoy mathematics
develop mathematical confidence
fill all math skill "holes"

Engaging Students Using Cooperative Learning, John Strebe © Taylor & Francis

Chapter 4

Collaborative Worksheets

Collaborative Worksheets

Often the first opportunity to earn **team points** involves doing a worksheet containing ideas and facts the students must learn and understand. The content could reflect the core learning goals found on state assessments, concepts needed by the students in a subsequent course or any skills determined to be important. The purpose for the worksheet is to encourage good thinking and learning. This is *not* a graded activity. I have heard from some educational experts that worksheets are destructive, boring and the use of them is a selfish, uncaring tool of a lazy teacher. I believe that the *traditional* worksheet method is what is deficient. That method usually included handing out the worksheets to students sitting in rows; students completing the worksheet; students finishing the worksheets and the teacher calling out the answers. Finally, the teacher asks if there are any questions. Using worksheets in this way can be boring with a minimum of profit.

Changing the structure of the classroom and teaching students how to productively interact with each other will make the use of a worksheet a dynamic and positive learning experience. For 12 years I did not do worksheets in the manner I will describe. It is embarrassing that I ignored the greatest resource found in any classroom—the students themselves. This method for maximizing the learning is called Respect-Defense-Consensus. It is actually an application of Think-Pair-Share (Lyman, 1987) to worksheet completion. The activities can be called RDC or 1-2-4 activities as described below:

Interactive Worksheet: "RDC" or "1-2-4"

Worksheets, readings, activity sheets, and practice tests *can be* useful to help students' mastery of skills and improvement in understanding. The way worksheets are used can be improved and made more effective. This change involves students talking to each other in pairs and small groups.

A few years ago, I wondered if the way I taught was in harmony with the way that I feel about students and, as a result, decided that a change was necessary. I wanted to respect *all* students, making sure that each student was actually learning. It was also my desire for each student to learn in a protected environment where embarrassment was minimized. In addition, it seemed important for the students to be asked to defend their conclusions so that the learning might be deepened. How could the above process be modified to satisfy these requirements? The following structure seems to satisfy some of my concerns.

	The "1" mode—Each student is provided with the written material and a
Respect	totally quiet environment for a measured amount of time. No sharing of information is done at this time.

	The "2" mode—Pairs of students discuss, compare, justify and defend their
Defense	conclusions. Consensus may or may not be achieved, but communication about the topic has been exhaustive. Changes in answers are optional. Each student speaks only with a partner.

	The "4" mode—Each pair confers with another pair about the conclusions and
Consensus	the logical support for them. Consensus is the goal, but not necessary.

Once these three modes have been used, the various perspectives are shared with the entire class; continued further discussion will clarify understanding. The manner of sharing can be selected to match the concepts being considered (Circle of Knowledge and simultaneous sharing with "erase and wipe" boards are two that I have found effective).

Notice that in the "1" Mode (Respect) each student is given equal access to the material without the interruption of others, and each person knows that accountability will follow in the "2" Mode. During the "2" Mode (Defense), silly answers are heard only by a partner, reducing their negative effect on the student and on the class. In addition, a less aggressive student can be protected against the domination by a more energetic one; this protection can be present in the "4" Mode (Consensus) as well. The effort at consensus encourages students to explain, defend and justify, allowing students to learn at a deeper level. Both the "2" mode and the "4" mode provide opportunities for the students to *rehearse* their explanations. This is especially important if students will be sharing conclusions with the entire class. It may be helpful to appoint a group "reporter" who will collect and summarize the group's efforts. Sometimes I ask students to *initial* the group consensus in order to have them take ownership of the result.

When deemed appropriate, this activity can be finished as a competition. Each team selects a captain who picks up a blank worksheet, returns to the team and conducts a team discussion resulting in "team answers." The captain has the power to select an answer when the team cannot decide. Team names are placed at the top of the team sheets and those same sheets are collected and graded after class by the teacher or exchanged with the papers of the other teams to be graded and discussed in class. A score is tallied for each team sheet, and the score is added to each team's score on the scoreboard. These grades do *not* appear in the grade book.

Respect Mode is vital, allowing each student to consider, reflect and decide without the influence of anyone, including the teacher. Original thought is encouraged, something which will later benefit the entire class. The goal is to have *every* student address the concepts being studied. It is often helpful for the teacher to roam the classroom during this time making sure that all students are engaged with the material.

Defense Mode is the *power* mode where pairs of students are encouraged to *justify, support, defend, explain, demonstrate or even prove their conclusions to be valid*. Having a list of these and other similar words in the classroom can be helpful; write them on a piece of newsprint and display for the entire class to see. During Defense Mode the emphasis is on discussion. Changes in conclusions which were reached during Respect Mode are optional, that is, a change can be made after an effective defense by a partner or the original conclusion can be kept. Each pair should refrain from communication with another pair at this time. I often use the nonverbal cue of each pair waving "goodbye" to the other pair in a team of four.

Careful pairing can allow even the most hesitant student to have the opportunity to speak. Pair this quiet student with someone who will be likely to listen. Putting together two students with dominant personalities can be productive. If a pair is struggling to discuss effectively, I will often help them to begin sharing by pulling up a chair and join them as a third partner. Once they are talking, the teacher is free to continue roaming the classroom. It is vital that students in pairs be taught to whisper to each other during this time. Of course, in teams of five, a pair of students and a trio of students would engage in discussion. At the close of Defense Mode having the students say "Thank you" to each other for sharing ideas creates a good habit as well as a productive class environment. After the Defense Mode, I will occasionally ask the students to raise their hands if any answers were changed. It continues to amaze me to see the number of raised hands, giving evidence of the learning that occurs when partners discuss.

During **Consensus Mode**, *team decisions* are made. Captains are encouraged to give everyone a fair audience to explain their thinking. Even shy students will share during this time because they have already rehearsed their explanations during the Defense Mode. Gaining confidence by receiving team approval, students are more likely to share their ideas later in front of the entire class.

To indicate that the team has reached consensus on all questions or at least determined team answers, each team is encouraged to *celebrate* with a "Strebe High One" or perhaps using another action that the team has created. Remember, doing a "Strebe High One" requires each member of the team to touch forefingers over the center of the group and make an arc while whispering "Yesssss."

If the papers are to be checked in class and if the answers are brief or even multiple choice, the choral answer method with the raised arm coming down after counting "1, 2, 3" can be used. A time for questions should be provided, although many questions have already been asked and answered in discussion with partners.

Notice that this is *not* a graded activity. The emphasis is on *learning*. Points can be assigned, but only toward team competition, not grades in the grade book. Respect, Defense, Consensus activities are effective in any subject area, for any level of difficulty and in any grade. Always adapt the strategy so it is appropriate for the particular situation where it is to be used.

After such an activity, team points can be written next to the team names beginning the soft team competition. Team points will continue to be earned by the teams using engaging learning activities. The competition will continue for an appropriate number of days until a quiz is given.

Individual Accountability

The quiz is taken without any collaboration. Kids may even sit in special quiz seats so that no two members from the same team sit near each other. **Individual accountability** is a key to developing a powerful interactive environment. The team quiz averages are added to the points already earned by the teams, and champions are crowned in each division.

Team competition with frequent championships seems to motivate students to work hard. Cooperation and competition can be blended together, as in team sports. Competition can be a positive asset, especially when competitive instincts are controlled, rather than in control. In addition, students should be encouraging and motivating their teammates to work and study. The collaborative classroom is a place where students have a great opportunity for success.

Chapter 5

Collaborative Review/Tests

Collaborative Review

Review of material seems to be an essential part of effective learning. Teachers are truly creative thinkers and use many wonderful ways to review. I have seen students play a classroom version of Jeopardy or Survivor. In some classes teams make up quiz questions to be used in a classroom team competition and then some of the questions are actually used on the quiz. Puzzle sheets can be used to keep the process from becoming tedious. One strategy I use is called **Pairs Check With a Switch**. Remember, it should be used to review familiar material.

Pairs Check With a Switch

The purpose of Pairs Check With a Switch is to encourage students to talk together about concepts being learned, to **review** material for a soon-to-be-given test. Sometimes students are hesitant to initiate conversation and will require an appropriate structure, such as this one, which encourages interaction. By using this activity the value of the concepts or problems being discussed is increased and kids are asked to justify the results of their thinking.

This activity requires that students choose partners or sit with partners assigned by the teacher. Each of the partners is designated by a color. One partner could be purple and the other gold.

Two different sheets of questions are prepared, one paper being designated "purple" and the other "gold." The problems on the "purple" sheet should be of the same difficulty and type as those on the "gold" sheet. For example, problem #1 on the purple sheet should be of the same domain as problem #1 on the gold; problem #2 on the purple should be similar to problem #2 on the gold. This pattern should continue throughout the papers. The papers should be constructed in parallel (sample sheets are provided later).

Next to each problem is a small diamond in which a check will be placed if a problem is worked correctly. Putting the Gold problems on one face of a paper and the Purple problems on the back allows students to practice skills at a later time.

When a trio of students is required, a third sheet can be prepared, such as "yellow" or two students in the trio can have the same sheet. When appropriate, the teacher can partner with the third student. The students seem to enjoy the fact that the teacher is doing the activity with them. I have found it advisable that when I do participate, to pick a student partner who is especially skilled with the material being reviewed. This allows me and my partner to finish before the others and for each of us to have the freedom to check and teach the rest of the class.

Procedure: Distribute the papers, asking one partner to turn the Gold side up and the other partner to turn the Purple side up.

When the teacher gives a signal:

1. Each partner works problem #1 on the sheet.

2. The partners signal each other with a nonverbal cue that problem #1 has been completed. (The signal should have been agreed upon before the activity began. Suggested signals—a look, thumbs up, a playing card turned face up.)

   I use **"the DONE look"** in my class because it adds fun to the activity. When explaining the strategy to the class I have the kids practice a look that says "I am done." It is truly fun. Often I have to remind the students that I did **not** say the "Dumb look." Much laughter can be heard at this time. We are working hard and having fun!

   Remember, learning should be the hardest work and the most fun we ever experience.

3. When both are finished working problem #1, the papers are exchanged and each partner checks the problem worked by the other person. If a problem is perceived as correct, a check should be placed in the box next to the problem. If a problem is perceived as incorrect, the pairs should discuss until the problem is understood and corrected and the box checked. *The person who wrote the incorrect answer should be the one to write the correct answer.* In this case, the student who is checking becomes a teacher. I instruct the students to *lead* their partner to the truth and to refrain from just supplying the correct response. Often I model this behavior prior to the class starting the activity.

   After a check is placed in the box, that partner gives exaggerated praise to the partner like, "You are the man," "You are the woman," or "You are awesome," or something similar. I ask the students to practice this before beginning the activity.

4. Do **NOT** exchange papers at this time.

5. Each partner now works problem #2. The Purple partner does #2 on the Gold sheet and the Gold partner does #2 on the Purple. When finished, each gives the other "the look."

6. Exchange papers and follow step 3. Do not forget the exaggerated praise.

7. Continue this procedure until all problems are completed. When a pair has completed the assignment, celebration should occur such as a silent "Strebe High 1." The celebration signals that they are ready to be checked.

Once a pair has completed the sheets, these can be checked using keys provided by the teacher. The teacher can pass out the keys to the finished pair or post several sets of keys in the room. The checked pair can then be used as checkers. They stay together and move around the classroom checking and teaching in the same way they have observed the teacher doing. Be sure that they have totally correct answers prior to checking other students. This pair will often find it necessary to teach.

By the close of the activity, several pairs of students will be checking other pairs. It is advisable for the teacher to have several sets of keys available.

The increased interaction that is generated by this activity deepens students' understanding of the academic subject and allows them to refine their social skills in an academic environment. The activity is fun for the students. I have had classes do this activity with much energy for over an hour, laughing and learning. I once used this activity for 70 minutes—it took quite a bit of time to create enough questions—to review for a final exam. The students remained engaged for the entire period and the exam grades for two classes were the highest I had ever experienced.

There are reasons for doing the activity in this way. I always have had a student who when given a worksheet will treat my signal to begin as if I had said, "Drivers, start your engines." That student will go "racing" through the sheet, finishing as fast as possible and slamming the pencil on the desk, indicating that a winner had been found. I call that student my "NASCAR Kid." Having students switch papers after each problem causes the students to stop, allowing the opportunity to *reflect* on the question or concept, requiring the students to *review* the concept as checking ensues. Reflection and review are key factors in learning. I do not want to rob even one student of these benefits.

Some of the academic concepts that I know best I learned because I taught someone else. Teaching another person cements the learning, deepens the understanding and increases retention. Having students teach the erring partner benefits both students. A vital component helping students to teach effectively is the observation of their teacher's quality teaching methods.

Someday most of our students will be a spouse or a parent and will perform better in those roles if praise is a perfected skill. After 39 years of marriage, my wife turned to me one day and said, "John, you have become a really good husband." I was glad she did not add, "finally." I kissed her and sincerely asked her if there was anything she needed to be done—anything! I was her man. Praise **is** powerful! A former principal of mine practiced the habit of visiting classrooms for 10 minutes, not to evaluate, but to observe, to see what was going on in the school. Later, after visiting my room he would find me and say something like, "Thanks for what you did today. We are blessed to have you in our school." I planned that night and came to school the next day with increased enthusiasm and energy—deserved, specific praise is effective!

Many of my students do not know how to praise because they have not experienced sufficient praise from those who should praise them—their parents, and embarrassingly for me, some of their teachers. **Pairs Check With a Switch** gives students the opportunity to practice and experience praise. They do a better job of this if they see it first modeled by me. The more kids praise each other, the better they get at praising. One day after doing this activity for about an hour in a freshman class, Shannon turned to her partner and said, "Tomika, your Momma did a good thing!" The class and I rolled with laughter as we realized the great thing her mother did was to have Tomika. Students enjoy doing this and I will hear from kids a request to do "that switch thing."

Some students have a strong desire to be a "NASCAR Kid," and in other classes they have been allowed, even trained to race through a review sheet. I always carry several blank sheets as I roam the classroom so I can collect and replace sheets when students have not switched, checked and reflected. I simply remind the students about why we are doing the activity and let them begin again.

The kids like to tell me I tricked them because they did twice as many problems as they had anticipated. Each student did every problem on both sheets. They are correct, but then they tell me how much fun it was to do.

Some Suggestions

When doing this activity for the first time, it may be necessary to keep the class together taking them through the activity step by step until they fully understand. With subsequent uses of Pairs Check With a Switch students will gain expertise and work independently.

A student who has missed class should be paired with a student who can teach using the purple and gold sheets. The teaching student could do #1 on the purple sheet and the returning student could demonstrate understanding by doing #1 on the gold sheet. This process could continue until all the questions were answered. After a period of time, the student who has returned from an absence may begin to understand the material and the activity can be finished from that point using the Pairs Check With a Switch procedure.

In some classes, especially with younger students, create the initial purple and gold sheets to be shorter with perhaps no more than five questions or examples to be considered.

Use this activity with all types of questions, not just short answer ones. In some classes the purple and gold sheets could have identical content. For example, in a literature class studying *Death of a Salesman*, question #1 on the purple and #1 on the gold could be something like, "Willy Loman planted a garden just prior to committing suicide. What could have been his purpose?" Each student may write a paragraph answer in explanation of Willy's motives. Each student could have written a valid response. After switching papers the reading and discussion of the different answers could result in a deepening of understanding for both students.

Several examples of Pairs Check With a Switch sheets are included here. Be creative and begin a file of sheets for your subject matter. In a few years you can have a substantial library of Pairs Check With a Switch sheets.

A Creative Signal

While conducting a teacher workshop in West Virginia, I was presenting the Pairs Check With a Switch strategy and remarked that kindergarten teachers should refrain from its use because the students would find the process too complex. During a return visit to the school I observed a talented kindergarten teacher, Kara Shuff, using Pairs Check With a Switch to review skills finding the sums of money. When a student finished a problem, that student would press down on a closet stick-up light to indicate to the partner that the problem had been completed. Half the students had blue lights and half had grey lights. If you are not impressed, then you have forgotten what it would be like to turn on a light during class when you were in kindergarten. The students loved this and no student was off task during the exercise. I have learned *never* to tell a kindergarten teacher that something is impossible!

GOLD

☐ 1. Evaluate $f(x) = -x^3$ if $x = -2$

☐ 2. $80 \div 4(5) = $ _____

☐ 3. $20 - 5 + 3 = $ _____

☐ 4. $\dfrac{10^{-2}}{10^{-6}} = $

☐ 5. Endpoints of a line segment in the plane are $(-10, 8)$ and $(14, -14)$. The midpoint has coordinates ( )

☐ 6. $6^4 \bullet 6^{-4} = $

☐ 7. $\dfrac{20 - 6}{10 - 3} = $

☐ 8. Find the radius of a circle whose equation is

$$(x - 2)^2 + (y + 4)^2 = 81$$

The radius is _____.

PURPLE

☐ 1. Evaluate $f(x) = -x^3$ *if* $x = -5$.

☐ 2. $60 \div 2(5) =$ _____

☐ 3. $30 - 6 + 4 =$ _____

☐ 4. $\dfrac{10^{-3}}{10^{-5}} =$

☐ 5. Endpoints of a line segment in the plane are (6,–4) and (10,–2). The midpoint has coordinates (   )

☐ 6. $8^{-2} \bullet 8^{2} =$

☐ 7. $\dfrac{30 + 6}{10 + 2} =$

☐ 8. Find the radius of a circle whose equation is

$$(x + 5)^2 + (y - 4)^2 = 64.$$

The radius is _____.

Pairs Check With a Switch
Geometry Facts

PURPLE

☐ 1. _____ angles total 180°

      A) Complementary   B) Supplementary

☐ 2. _____ triangles have 2 equal sides

      A) Scalene   B) Isosceles

☐ 3. Skew lines _____ meet in a point

      A) Sometimes   B) Never

☐ 4. The four angles of a quadrilateral always total _____°.

☐ 5. List 3 different types of quadrilaterals.

      1) _____

      2) _____

      3) _____

Pairs Check With a Switch
Geometry Facts

GOLD

☐ 1. _____ angles total 90°

       A) Complementary   B) Supplementary

☐ 2. _____ triangles have no equal sides

       A) Scalene   B) Isosceles

☐ 3. Parallel lines _____ meet in a point.

       A) Sometimes   B) Never

☐ 4. The three angles of a triangle always total _____.

☐ 5. List 3 different types of triangles.

       1) _____

       2) _____

       3) _____

Engaging Students Using Cooperative Learning, John Strebe © Taylor & Francis

Pairs Check With a Switch

Name_____

4th grade review

Date_____

Computation and Estimation (1)

BLACK

 What is the sum of 1,292 and 1,379 ?

F   2,661

G   2,671

H   2,681

J   2,761

 Which of the following best describes the difference 43,441–35,184 ?

A   Closer to 10,000 than 8,000

B   Closer to 10,000 than 9,000

C   Closer to 9,000 than 8,000

D   Closer to 8,000 than 7,000

 Ada took a three-day driving trip. She drove 425 miles the first day, 378 miles the second day, and 539 miles the third day. About how many miles did Ada drive in the three days?

F   700 miles

G   800 miles

H   1,300 miles

J   1,500 miles

 $43.69

–$ 5.77

A $37.92

B $38.92

C $42.12

D $49.46

Pairs Check With a Switch

Name_____

4th grade review

Date_____

Computation and Estimation (1)

<u>GOLD</u>

 What is the difference between 112,841 and 92,408?

A   20,433
B   20,443
C   20,447
D   20,449

 Which *best* describes the difference 3,021-987?

F   Closer to 1,000 than 2,000
G   Closer to 2,000 than 3,000
H   Closer to 4,000 than 3,000
J   Closer to 5,000 than 4,000

 Sam spent $3.29 for an ice cream sundae and $0.98 for a drink. What is the total amount Sam spent for the ice cream sundae and drink?

F $3.27
G $4.17
H $4.27
J $4.37

 34.6–2.82 =

F   16.4
G   31.78
H   33.22
J   33.78

Engaging Students Using Cooperative Learning, John Strebe © Taylor & Francis

PURPLE

1. Willy Loman planted a garden prior to taking his life. Discuss the significance of the garden.

2. How was Happy's personality shaped by his parents' lives?

3. Discuss the role of Willy's wife in the family struggles.

GOLD

1.   Willy Loman planted a garden prior to taking his life. Discuss the significance of the garden.

2.   How was Biff's personality shaped by his parents' lives?

3.   Discuss the role of Willy in the family struggles.

Engaging Students Using Cooperative Learning, John Strebe © Taylor & Francis

PURPLE

Supply the OPPOSITE from the list of words at the bottom of the paper.

Δ   1. beautiful   _____

Δ   2. light   _____

Δ   3. fat   _____

Δ   4. small   _____

Δ   5. soft   _____

Δ   6. wet   _____

Δ   7. tall   _____

Δ   8. fast   _____

Δ   9. sweet   _____

Δ   10. loud   _____

new/smooth/slow/shallow/cold/ugly/sour/dull/mean/
dirty/dry/thin/last/quiet/large/short/lazy/dark/hard/light

GOLD

Supply the OPPOSITE from the list of words at the bottom of the paper.

Δ   1.   hot   _____

Δ   2.   shiny   _____

Δ   3.   first   _____

Δ   4.   energetic   _____

Δ   5.   deep   _____

Δ   6.   nice   _____

Δ   7.   clean   _____

Δ   8.   old   _____

Δ   9.   heavy   _____

Δ   10.   rough   _____

new/smooth/slow/shallow/cold/ugly/sour/dull/mean/dirty/
dry/thin/last/quiet/large/short/lazy/dark/hard/light

BLUE

In each case a word is incorrectly spelled. Using the word bank at the bottom of the page choose the correct spelling and write that in the space provided:

Δ   1.   xmi   _____

Δ   2.   stla   _____

Δ   3.   ktich   _____

Δ   4.   lemsl   _____

Δ   5.   enfird   _____

Δ   6.   nesd   _____

Δ   7.   celnag   _____

Word Bank

friend   smell   last   glance

thick   mix   send

SILVER

In each case a word is incorrectly spelled. Using the word bank at the bottom of the page choose the correct spelling and write that in the space provided:

Δ   1.   limk   _____

Δ   2.   eahd   _____

Δ   3.   ktics   _____

Δ   4.   flte   _____

Δ   5.   nith   _____

Δ   6.   lsacs   _____

Δ   7.   ypemt   _____

Word Bank

left	thin	ticks	head
class	milk	empty	

Engaging Students Using Cooperative Learning, John Strebe © Taylor & Francis

High Stakes Exams

In recent years much emphasis has been placed on students performing well when taking high stakes exams, whether they are exams for graduation, AP tests or school system benchmark evaluations. I began to use something I call **1 – 4 Competition Quiz/Review** and have observed a significant increase in the number of students passing these tests.

1 – 4
Team Competition
Quiz/Review

An activity which has increased the number of students doing serious review for final exams has been the 1 – 4 structure. Each student is given a review sheet or activity involving opportunities to consider material studied throughout the year. The review should reflect the content and the form of the exams to be taken. If the systemwide exams are primarily multiple choice in nature, the review should be created in multiple choice format. If brief or extended constructive response describes the form of the exams, then the review should reflect that form of question.

During the **"1" mode** each student works in silence; collaboration is not permitted while each student's individual thought time is respected. In order to encourage individual thinking, student desks are separated. Students should be allowed the same resources on the review that will be allowed on the exam; for example, students might be investigating with the computer or working at learning stations.

At an appropriate time, the students are instructed to form their collaborative teams. The **"4" mode** requires the group to thoroughly discuss the review assignment with emphasis on the words *justify, explain, defend, prove* or *demonstrate*. For best results, the teams should have been formed by the teacher into groups that are the most likely to produce excellence. In addition, some engaging team building will contribute to more effective team interaction. A captain is appointed and given a blank review sheet. The captain puts the team name on the top of the sheet and conducts a group discussion resulting in team consensus and the team answer sheet is completed. This discussion is often very powerful, resulting in one student working out analysis for the other team members in order to convince them of a particular result. The captain is required to make a final team decision when a compromise cannot be achieved. During this process the teacher needs to move through the classroom encouraging the participation of all students.

When all teams have completed the activity, the team answer sheets are exchanged and the correct answers are provided in class, or the team sheets are collected and graded by the teacher prior to the next class. The team with the best performance is awarded a set number of team competition points. A winner can be determined and rewarded for just this competition, or the points can be added to the team totals during an ongoing competition and tangible rewards can be given when appropriate. Tangible team rewards are objects the teacher has determined are appropriate, that the students would like, that the teacher can afford and that the school allows.

Initially, a winning team might need to get only 20 out of 25 questions correct; however, as this strategy is used repeatedly, team competition has an impact and eventually a score below 24 or 25 out of 25 will not be sufficient to win. Using the 1 – 4 every few weeks, each time with a new review sheet, prepares the students for the actual exam. Subsequent review sheets should reflect additional skills taught as well as missed questions from previous review sheets. The power of this strategy comes when students engage by discussing with each other as they justify and defend. Competition incites students to do this thoroughly; teams that are well formed and strongly built will devote all their energy to being #1.

Students should check their individual papers and reflect on how team decisions were made, especially when team answers were incorrect and individual answers were correct. Opportunity for reflection can be provided by instructing the students to be in **Respect Mode**. During this time the teacher can direct the reflection. The result is that many students are more persuasive the next time the activity is used. In addition, I have seen students gain the respect of other students, especially when their correct answers had been rejected by the team.

1 – 4 Team Competition Quiz/Review can be used when giving a quiz. When this is desired, each student is encouraged to write quiz answers on a plain sheet of paper as well as on the quiz paper during the "1" mode. So, each student writes each answer *twice.* When the "1" mode activity is completed, the plain sheet of paper, which now contains the answers, should be collected for grading and recording by the teacher. The students keep the quiz paper with the written questions and their answers. It is important to remember that the teacher has collected the quizzes to be graded later and grades to be recorded and that the student responses were made *without* any collaboration with teammates.

The captains now come to the teacher and are given another copy of the quiz to be used to achieve team consensus. As the **"4" mode** begins, spirited team discussion comments like, "O man, I missed that one and now I see why" are heard repeatedly. The kids are discovering what they did right and wrong on the quiz within minutes after submitting their quizzes rather than one or two days later. In many cases, students are teaching other students how correct thinking should have occurred or "high fiving" each other for good thinking. I am constantly amazed at how energetically the team sheets containing team answers are completed.

Simple team competition with simple team rewards motivates this dynamic interaction. The extended block period allows the time for this to occur. If the same quiz will be given to another class later in the day, collect all materials to be returned to the students at a later time. If the quiz should require the entire class period, do the "4" mode the next day with a team captain just prior to returning the graded quizzes. Most student questions will have been answered before the class discussion of the quiz.

Occasionally, but rarely, students are allowed to keep their quiz answer sheets until after the team discussion. They are permitted to change any answer they wish before handing in their quiz sheets. Students should be reminded to change only answers that they are logically convinced were incorrect. In this case, the individual answer sheets may not agree with the team consensus sheet. Such an approach could be used the first time this activity is done to emphasize the value of the collaboration.

Collecting answer sheets *prior* to collaboration and grading them puts increased value on each individual's performance, discouraging the practice of a student relying on another person instead of working diligently themselves. After the teacher grades the quizzes, the team quiz average can be added to the team point totals the next day.

If students ask whether papers are to be collected before or after collaboration, a less than definitive answer may be the best response in order to encourage all students to give a genuine effort on each exercise during the "1" mode. Remember to preserve **individual accountability** on most quizzes.

My experience after using this strategy was that students performed radically higher on high stakes, end-of-year exams than students in other classes or from other schools.

To properly prepare students for the high stakes exams, this activity needs to be used periodically throughout the year. When students take the actual exam they tend to feel comfortable with it because they have had many similar **1 – 4 Team Competition Quiz/Review** experiences as preparation.

Quiz Seats

Suppose you create cooperative teams in your classroom that generate much enthusiasm to be the highest performing team in the class. Haven't you also increased the incentive to achieve results in any way possible, even cheating? Reducing temptation can be effectively done by giving the students new seats during the quiz. One approach that helps to preserve integrity in the classroom is to assign **Quiz Seats,** a seating arrangement where students can still sit in groups, but no one from their "home" team sits in that group. Since the students are not sitting with their own team, they will be very protective of their work, even careful to use a cover sheet as they take a test or quiz. After all, allowing others to copy would be to reduce their team's chances at winning.

One effective way to assign quiz seats is described here:

♦ In each team the people count off 1, 2, 3, 4, 5 so each person on the team has been assigned exactly one number.

♦ Establish a path in the classroom passing through each team. In my room I might start at team #2, going to team #3, then #4 and so forth (numbers hanging above each group) through each team until the path comes back to the starting point.

♦ Ask all the #1's to stand up with their pencils, cover sheets and personal items. Announce a direction, perhaps clockwise, and instruct each student who is a #1 to move one group on the path and sit down.

♦ Now have all the students who have been assigned #2 to stand with their materials. Ask them to say out loud, "Skip. Sit." These students move on the path skipping the first group encountered and sitting in the next group, walking clockwise.

♦ The #3's stand and say, "Skip. Skip. Sit," and then move clockwise on the path skipping two groups and sitting in the next group.

♦ The #4's are instructed to stand up and then to sit down right where they are presently sitting.

♦ The #5's will sit together in a new group or they can be scattered around the room. They should not sit with members of their "home" team.

Once the students are in their **Quiz Seats**, ask them to return to their home teams. Now make it a competition to see how quickly the class can reorganize to the quiz seats. Telling them that first period did this in 20 seconds can motivate. I have timed 30 ninth-graders taking 6 seconds to get to their new seats after I tell them, "Go!" Please instruct them to carry their pencils point down and to take the shortest path to their new seats.

The assignment of quiz seats needs to be done whenever new teams are created; for me it would be about every 8–10 weeks in an alternating block schedule.

After the quiz answers have been collected the kids can return to their home teams with their quiz papers on which answers are written and do the **1 – 4 Team Competition Quiz/Review**. Be sure to collect all papers prior to the close of class. Another possibility would be to teach a mini-lesson to the students while they are in their quiz seats.

Stir Seats

After years of teaching, I have developed the ability to sense even before the late bell sounds when a particular class period is going to be a challenge. There is just something in the air. At that moment I instruct the students not to unpack their books and at a particular moment give them a signal sending them to their quiz seats. Students will say, "We didn't know we were having a quiz today. That's not fair." I tell them they are correct and we are not having a quiz today. Then I proceed with the lesson plan for the day. What occurs is some of the best learning we have experienced in days. The classroom has been refreshed and the Quiz Seats have become the **Stir Seats** (Kagan, 1995).

All classes can become stagnant at times and "stirring" the class refreshes everyone. In this new arrangement students are not sure how much acting out this new team will endure so focus tends to be better. Sometimes I will stir the class for a single activity like the Defense Mode for a worksheet, returning the students to their home team for the Consensus Mode. Occasionally the students will sit in their Stir Seats for 2 days until it is time to "Go home again." You are the expert and will know the appropriate time to leave the students in these new seats. When the kids rejoin their teams, it is as if they have been on a trip, and they are usually happy to be back together.

Team Rewards

After a period of time when team points have accumulated, I announce that after a particular activity, usually a test or quiz, champions in each division would be crowned. Rewards and recognition are given to the outstanding teams. What can be used for team rewards? Anything you and the students decide is desirable, affordable and appropriate. For many years I distributed Tootsie Pops, one to each member of the top-performing teams. It is wise to have alternate rewards—such as pencils or pens—for students who cannot have the candy. Some school systems have barred the giving of candy so other rewards must be used. In elementary school the students from the winning teams are allowed to wear paper crowns which they have made themselves. I have an old basketball trophy that stands about 3.5 feet tall and each winning team takes turns having it sit in the middle of the team so anyone walking in the door notices that team first.

In my classroom I always have a **Wall of Fame** where the photographs of the winning teams are placed. For years I have used a Polaroid camera which gives immediate results. I have the students sign the bottom of the champion's picture before putting it on the wall of fame. Some teachers are doing this with the digital cameras getting beautiful pictures from the computer.

When floating as a teacher, I use pieces of shower board, white board sold in 4 by 8 foot pieces at a home improvement supply store, as the sites for the wall of fame. The store cut each board into thirds. The pictures are taped to the board, which is placed on the chalk tray during class. At the close of class the board can be stored behind a file cabinet. Team names can also be placed on one of these boards. At the close of the year, I give the pictures to students to take home as part of their memories of a good year at school.

Be creative with rewards but always give *team rewards*, not individual rewards. Ask the students what they think would make a good reward, but be careful. One team chose to attend a basketball game with me and then go out to dinner with me and my wife. We had a memorable evening that we all treasure. For dessert one of the student's mothers brought an ice cream cake complete with a quadratic equation written in the icing. The kids solved the equation on their napkins while enjoying the delicious cake. Of course, the parents submitted written permission for this activity and the teacher had the resources for it to occur. Rewards that cost no money and are always available can be categorized as "special privilege." The winning team leaves for lunch or for the bus first. The champions might be allowed to wear a hat in class. The winners could relocate their team to a special area of the class to sit for the week. The champions could tutor students from a different classroom.

Generally, use rewards appropriate for students and for the situation. Rewards can be simple—such as lunch with the teacher. If the school permits, the teacher could bring fresh vegetables or fruit or some other treat to share. Each teacher will determine the best rewards in each case.

Chapter 6

Interactive Lecture

Interactive Lecture

There are many myths about a collaboratively structured classroom. One is that there is no lecture in a truly cooperative setting. Many teachers are dynamic, instructive, entertaining and skilled at presenting engaging lectures. I have had students at the close of a lecture remain in their seats by their own choice when the bell rings, letting the truths they had just heard "sink in" and as they left class telling me that the lecture was amazing, shaking my hand and expressing thanks. Even the most gifted lecturer does not "capture" everyone during the class; engaging *every* student is the goal. I have discovered that during every class there are several major questions. They are often introductory, transitional, discovery or summary in nature and are offered by the teacher as well as students in the class. How we handle these *key* questions can influence how well we engage the students in the class.

My friend, Dr. Frank Lyman, taught me the first steps in this process. He is the intelligent and creative thinker responsible for the categories that I use here to describe student and teacher behavior in the asking of *key* questions. I am constantly thankful for his valuable insights into student engagement. What I am about to describe is logical and simple to understand. I learned these concepts sitting in a hallway listening to Frank teach a group of teachers how to do this even though I was not part of that group and could not even see Frank as he taught. Acquiring the discipline to effectively use these strategies requires commitment, time and practice, but what helped me to persevere was the realization that interactive lecture is very good for students.

Think/Pair/Square/Share

My students come to me not knowing how to fully engage in the consideration of a key question, so I must intentionally teach them how this is done. First, I must consider the necessary changes in my own behavior and then believe that the investment in time and energy to train my students is justified by the result. After 26 years of handling key questions in the manner described here, I am committed to asking major questions in only this way.

If I should ask a class, "Who was the 16th president of the United States," I am likely to see hands raised around the room, some of them energetically waving for recognition. I may hear several students whisper or shout out the answer. Some students are not sure or they have no idea about the answer to the question, but the class environment is not conducive to their continuing to think about or deduce the correct answer. This is even more true for a deeper analytical question. If I offer a clue such as providing an event

61

from that president's administration, more energetic hand waving and louder responses are likely to occur. This approach is not respectful of all students, but it was the way I was taught and is the manner in which I asked key questions of my classes for 12 years.

Think Mode

Now I teach my students **Think Mode** and indicate that we are in Think Mode by a nonverbal cue; for me it is pointing at my head. My students learn that when they see that cue or hear me say, "We are in Think Mode" the following behaviors are expected:

All communication stops (including lip-synching).

No shouting out of answers is allowed.

You may write, but do not show anyone what you wrote.

You may use a calculator.

You may use acceptable resources.

No hands should be raised.

Think, but tell no one what you are thinking, not even a whisper.

Students will raise their hands, especially when first learning **Think Mode**. In order not to disturb students' thinking by verbally instructing them to "Lower your hands," I use a nonverbal cue of reaching out with both arms, hands open, parallel to the floor and repeatedly lowering my arms. Students with their hands up are usually looking at the teacher and when they observe this cue they always lower their hands helping to create a nonpressure environment for thinking. Students still working on the question are not even aware that I have motioned for hands to be lowered.

The students stay in this mode for a period of time determined by the teacher. Obviously, the amount of *wait time* used will vary and depend on the nature of the question asked. For instance, if we were studying *A Separate Peace*, I might ask why Finny jounced the limb causing Gene to fall? Such a question may require more time for proper reflection, perhaps an opportunity to write a response. When introducing **Think Mode**, it helps for the teacher to walk around the classroom with a finger held to the lips indicating silence or perhaps with both hands held palms out indicating not to share with another person. Sometimes, repeated whispered "sshhssing" works.

Every student is vital. Every student deserves the opportunity to consider the question in a quiet environment, unbiased by the input of another person, especially that of the teacher.

Another key factor to encourage **Think Mode** is for the teacher to change the way a question is asked. When a teacher asks, "Who was the 16th president of the United States of America," of course hands will go up and vocal responses will be heard. In order to discourage the shouting out of answers and distracting hand-raising I found I needed to change my question to a statement, "***Let's just think*** about presidents." Not one student shouts out and not one hand is raised. Next, I said, "***Let's think about*** the 16th president of the USA. *Just think*." Again, students stayed in **Think Mode**. The teacher needs to put away "Who is?," "Which one?," "Why did?" and all other questions that beg and bait the students to answer. We are hoping to encourage thinking. After good thinking, answers will come during the **Pair Mode, Square Mode** and **Share Mode**. Start practicing, "*Let's think about*" and you will hear more thoughtful responses from your students.

The students are then taught **Pair Mode** where they begin by giving their prearranged partner a "high five" and then are encouraged to discuss the question with that partner. The "high five" physically and visually identifies the partners for the students' and for the teacher's benefit. I have found this physical identification to be a crucial step. **Pair Mode** is also called "Whisper Mode," describing the voice to be used.

Pair Mode

During **Pair Mode** the students:

Share their answers.

Justify, support, defend, explain, and demonstrate their answers.

Thank each other for the sharing.

Decide whether or not to change the original answer (remember that consensus is not the goal and changes are optional.)

Never talk with another pair.

My nonverbal cue is to hold up 2 fingers on one hand. During this mode students rehearse their responses to the question, each trying explanations out on another person in a nonthreatening environment. Even the most shy student can share with confidence in this protected setting, especially if the teacher has purposefully created the pairs.

Using **Pair Mode** can lessen potential embarrassment in front of an entire class when a silly or wrong answer is expressed. That same incorrect answer is dismissed in quiet, usually by a familiar and trusted partner. Students who have been humiliated in front of an entire class often will be very hesitant when asked to share in the future; that is why I sometimes call **Pair Mode** the "Protection Mode." Genuine engagement occurs when students are talking with other students about academic material. Class clowns are short circuited in their quest for attention by reducing the audience for their sensational answers. Instead of entertaining the entire class, the clown shares the silliness with only one person, making it not so much fun to be a dummy. During this time, the students are aware that the roaming teacher is listening to their discussion. Properly executed, this gives the teacher the opportunity to bond as well as to evaluate.

Why should a student think about the question during **Think Mode** anyway? Out of 30 students, the probability of being called on by the teacher is fairly low. In a classroom that has been trained in **Pair Mode** questioning, *every* student will be asked what he or she thinks about the key question by a partner. That is why I also refer to **Pair Mode** as the "Accountability Mode." In such a setting, the probability of being called on is 1; it is a certainty! (Don't you just love this?)

Square Mode

Enlarging the audience to 4 students happens during **Square Mode** where two pairs of students get together to talk about the question. My nonverbal cue is my arm extended with a finger pointed down and my hand making a circular motion. Make sure that during this mode each member of a group of students is spatially close to each other member of the group. Desks should be moved together and students encouraged to lean toward a center point.

During **Square Mode**:

No hands are raised.

Much discussion is done.

No shouting out occurs.

Every student's thinking is respected.

A captain can be appointed to facilitate discussion, giving a structure for the response.

Consensus *can* be the goal, but engaging together is the objective.

One thing I have noticed is that students are more likely to share because they have already rehearsed and tried out their thinking on a partner, becoming confident in their thinking or streamlining their explanations with the help of their partner.

Some students process slower than others and this way of addressing a question allows most students to give a more complete consideration by "catching up" during pair or square time. Refining of conclusions will occur due to the increased time and because of the different perspectives offered by the partners. The intense pressure is lessened, allowing for a greater number of students to address the question.

Share Mode

At an appropriate time I will raise my hand indicating we are now in **Share Mode**, when the results of thinking will be shared with the entire class. One powerful way to conduct **Share Mode** is to give each group an erase/wipe board, a pen, a paper towel and appoint a "board writer" whose job it is to write the conclusions of the group on the board. The teacher can say a simple command such as "Boards up" and require that all boards be raised in the air within half a second for everyone to see the team answers. Sometimes I will ask the class for a "magic word" which I will repeat every time I want the boards up. The kids enjoy this word that they suggest, adding to the fun of the learning. Words like "lollapalusa" or "whamm-o" or the name of a favorite college are often suggested.

Remember—learning should be the hardest work we ever do and the most fun!

Another profitable way to receive feedback from the class is to allow a "reporter" from each group to offer a short response for the class to hear. One group begins and then each group contributes in order around the classroom. Some people refer to this form of response as "Circle of Knowledge."

Treating key questions in this manner allows more students to engage in the question, helps to deepen the thinking and provides an increased number of approaches to the question. If there are 30 students in the class, I want 30 students to consider and discuss the question, not just the one unlucky soul who got called on by the teacher—you know, the one who forgot and made the mistake of making eye contact with the teacher.

Introduction of Think, Pair, Square, Share

When introducing this to a class, help the students to realize that **Think/Pair/Square/ Share** is really *for them*. I use competition to help them see the importance and the effectiveness of each mode. With pairs and squares of students identified and "erase and wipe" response boards distributed, the class is put into **Think Mode** and a rebus example is shown to the class, something like

```
HEAD
HEELS
```

The students are asked to think of an English phrase with the help of the rebus.

After some time has passed, the students are instructed to talk to a partner about the rebus solution. At this time, it is vital to restrict the sharing between pairs. One pair should *not* talk with another pair, even if the two people have no idea about the conclusion.

Square Mode begins when two pairs rejoin to form a team of four and a consensus response is determined and written on an "erase and wipe" board. The class has been told that each team with a correct response on the board *after* **Square Mode** will be given 5 points (a correct response for the included rebus would be "head over heels"). This process is repeated up to four additional times with the points earned by each group accumulating. At the close of the activity the winning teams are recognized and the class has learned how key questions will be handled. The students have a valuable new learning tool and they enjoyed acquiring it. Selecting rebus examples appropriate for each class is vital. Have several rebus sets of varying difficulty available when conducting this activity. One supply of rebus examples can be found at *http://kids.niehs.nih.gov/ braintpics.htm.*

In addition to students writing the answer to a question on the erase-and-wipe-board for 5 points, I now encourage them to write any truth as well, such as, "Today is Monday" or "It is cold outside" or "Mr. Strebe is cool" or "The Blue Devils are the best." If the answer to the rebus or the question should be incorrect, instead of earning no points, they are given, say, 2 points for the truth. If the answer to the question is correct, they are given the 5 points and no points for the truth. It is better if all teams can earn some points in each case. I can remember some of my prouder students who would tell me that they were not going to put a truth down, being so confident in their answer. Sometimes their answer was wrong and they received no points by their own choice. Not putting down a truth is called, "Flying Naked" and is definitely not recommended. The truth is the *backup answer* which allows no group to be shut out; supplying a truth is fun and lightens the mood in the classroom.

Take this marvelous tool **Think, Pair, Square, Share** and adapt it to your situation. It works anywhere. I remember seeing a film of a first grade teacher using **Think/Pair/Share** to develop a list of safety rules. The students were sitting as informal pairs on a rug with no desks or chairs. The teacher wore a spinner attached to a cloth necklace. The disk had three sectors, each with one or more "Grovers" drawn. The first was a single Grover pointing at his head. The second was a drawing of two Grovers speaking to each other and the third had several Grovers with hands in the air. As the teacher moved the spinner, the little kids were pensive, then actively engaged in pair discussion and finally enthusiastically raising their hands. I do not use the Grover wheel in high school, but how very appropriate it is for elementary students. Remember—*Adapt, Create, Renew.*

Think/Pair/Square/Share is brilliant and once you use it you will be addicted. To see so many students actively engaged is thrilling. I soon discovered that it was not only a learning tool, but a *class management* structure as well. So much is earned from the investment of training a class to do this. As the year continues, *retraining a class is often necessary*, because kids forget and so do teachers; the retraining can serve as a good team builder as well.

Be Creative with Interactive Lecture

Each of the 4 modes can stand alone. The 4 modes can be creatively sequenced depending on the situation. Sometimes using **Square Mode** first is appropriate to get kids talking. Then follow up with **Think Mode** and **Pair Mode** and another **Square Mode**. I had an "aha" moment one day when I realized after a key question was processed that perhaps 40% of my students had not truly understood what had been discussed. It was then I realized that an opportunity to reflect upon what had been analyzed was necessary before going on. The sequence looks like this:

Think/Pair/Square/Share/Reflect (really an additional Think Mode)

During this time students can be reminded to look at the board where truths have been written or verbally reminded about cogent points during the discussion. Frank Lyman calls this reflection a "second think time."

The wheel helps me to remember not to get caught in a monotonous rut:

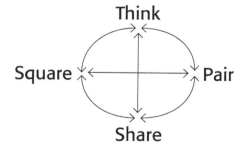

The different modes of TPSS are represented in the diagram. The arrows illustrate that the movement from a given mode may be to any of the other modes. Below are some possible paths to learning:

Think/Pair/Share	the most simple approach, requires pairs
Think/Square/Share	extension to teams, requires teams
Think/Pair/Square/Share	offers more protection and increases interaction, requires pairs within teams
Think/Pair/Share/Think	students reflect on the conclusions, requires pairs (second think time)
Think/Pair/Square/Share/Think	extends the preceding path, requires pairs and teams (second think time)
Think/Share	makes sure everybody is thinking
Think/Pair/Think/Pair/Share	used for tough questions with clues given during second think time, requires pairs
Square/Think/Pair/Square/Share	allows students to refine original thoughts
Share/Think/Pair/Share	the share time is brainstorming with the class, followed by reflection and pair discussion
Think/Pair/Pairs Visit Another Pair/Square/Share	promotes interaction in the classroom
Think/Pair	everyone thinks, everyone is accountable

BE CREATIVE AND INNOVATE!
HAVE COURAGE!

Help students to understand that using **Think/Pair/Square/Share** benefits them. This is a strategy that is student friendly, providing respect, protection and safety. The teacher also benefits from the increased opportunity to observe, analyze and make decisions about the learning environment. Using this structure is pleasantly addictive. Try it and enjoy!

Team Feedback

One of the goals of the collaborative classroom is to encourage all students to engage in learning. Student thought needs to be valued and student response heard. One way to do this efficiently is **Circle of Knowledge** (Dunn & Dunn, 1978).

Circle of Knowledge

This structure can be used to:

a. Allow for all students to contribute.

b. Brainstorm new ideas.

c. Review what was taught today.

d. Cause students to intensify on one subject.

e. Develop a study guide or list of facts.

f. Encourage students not to hide their ideas.

g. Generate sample test questions.

To use the activity:

a. Form the class into small groups of 3 or more students.

b. Present the students with a topic or a question.

c. Provide time (Think Time) to write a number of facts, ideas or questions.

d. Establish a person to begin the circle (perhaps the person wearing the most blue).

e. Decide to move on the circle clockwise or counterclockwise.

f. Each person shares one fact or idea in turn moving around the circle.

g. Agree that the same idea or fact may be shared once only.

h. Agree that when a person has exhausted his or her ideas, the word "pass" can be used to move on to the next person.

i. As an idea or fact is shared each person looks at his or her own list and puts a check by the idea or fact shared. If the item shared is not on the list, each person adds that fact to the bottom of the list. Everyone in the group will have the same list at the close of the activity.

Now do the activity with each group in the class being a point on the circle. Each group shares one idea, fact or question around the room. Checking and adding to the list allows each person to have a complete list.

At a certain point in the process, random sharing can be initiated to exhaust the ideas. Doing **Circle of Knowledge** in teams is just the structuring of **Pair Mode** and doing the **Circle of Knowledge** in the class structures the **Share Mode**. Introduce creative changes and additions to fit your purpose.

One way to ensure that each student is participating is to have each team assign a number to each team member starting with #1 and numbering in order until each person on the team has a number. A 4-member team would use the numbers #1, #2, #3, and #4. As the teacher circles around the class from team to team hearing answers, the responding student can be requested by saying which number student is to answer aloud. The students do not know ahead of time which number is going to be called; all students are thereby motivated to stay focused.

Sometimes one creative idea can allow us to experience a new freedom in our teaching. We need to be unafraid to try new practices, techniques and strategies that we believe will be good for us and for our students. When new ideas are tried, often failure is the result, but if we tried them because *we believed in them,* we will fix them and try them again. Soon we will have new treasures for our classroom. We teachers need to be *free to fail* so that we can improve. When I was learning to have a collaborative classroom, I was blessed with an administrator for whom instruction was the #1 priority. He gave me the opportunity to learn new things and a safe, nonthreatening environment in which to gain new skills. I will always give thanks for my principal, Dr. Edgar Markley, who treated me as a professional and gave me the freedom to grow.

We can learn new ideas anywhere. I remember how years ago I was sitting in that hallway waiting to present some ideas about team learning to a group of teachers at our staff development center. The group inside was hearing a presentation by Dr. Frank Lyman about Think/Pair/Share, but I was not part of the class. As I wrote earlier, I could not even see Frank, but what he said made sense and I took it back to my classroom. Be ready at all times to learn to be a more effective teacher. My sincere hope is that by taking the time to read this book, you and your students will benefit.

Chapter 7

Key Ideas

Key Ideas

Educational Interrupters
Pairs Ask Quickly
Unique and Valuable
Player/Coach
Student Enforcers

Educational Interrupters

I have had the wonderful opportunity to teach in three different block schedules as well as the traditional 6- and 7-period days. In each of these settings some of my students would drift mentally, but especially in the 90-minute classes. I remember speaking in contrived voices, changing my pitch and accent in order to get students' attention. A fellow teacher kept his 8 o'clock morning class on the edge of their seats by hopping up on his teacher's desk and teaching while walking the edge of the desk. The students paid rapt attention in case he were to fall; no one wanted to miss that! Once while teaching in a large city school on a hot June day in a classroom without air conditioning—go figure— I was overcome by the heat and instead of fainting, I sat down quickly on the floor just below the chalkboard on which I had been writing. From the students' view I had just disappeared from sight. One of my students wondered aloud if I were attempting to get their attention. We have all tried such antics in the classroom and many of them work quite well.

While observing my drifting students one day, I thought that what was needed were **Educational Interrupters**, activities which had an educational purpose that would interrupt the daydreaming, thought-wandering student. An educational interrupter can be the change from the teacher directing the learning to students doing the teaching, having students pick up needed materials, changing seat assignments from normal by "stirring the class" or any activity which has an educational purpose and also requires the students to alter present behavior.

Most years I was assigned two classes where the majority of students had been diagnosed with learning disabilities. For several years I was blessed with Michelle Mann as my resource teacher. We developed a tag team approach to teaching these classes: one of us would teach for approximately 7 minutes and then hand off the teaching responsibility to the other. The change in teacher was the educational interrupter and was

73

positive for all students, but especially those who were beginning to disengage. It was also beneficial for the teachers. (This was possible because Michelle knew mathematics, had teaching skill and desired to help the students learn.)

Sometimes we would let a student hold a timer with 7 minutes entered on the display and instruct until the buzzer went off. Kids felt they were controlling the class. In this case, when a student's behavior distracted from the learning, the timer was stopped and not restarted until the behavior changed. Other kids, when they realized that this misbehaving student was prolonging the segment, encouraged the student to straighten up. Having a student operate the clock provided an effective interrupter for the class.

The need for interrupters becomes very clear upon a visit to a 90- minute *lecture only* class. For students in such classes the change from 50- minute classes to 90-minute classes changed the classroom from a good place to sleep to one where you could expire without anyone noticing the event. Even a good lecturer's class will profit from educational interrupters. The use of **Think/Pair/Square/Share** has built-in interrupters that enhance a lecture. For example, going to **Think Mode**, sometimes with writing, causes students to engage because each knows that a partner will soon hold him or her accountable for the thinking.

Students seem especially focused in many classes during the first 15 minutes of a given class. Taking advantage of this, I would often begin class with a learning activity, which could be an interactive lecture, a pairs investigation or some other engaging strategy. Often I would use the checking of homework as the first interrupter. The effective use of educational interrupters throughout a class period can radically improve the efficiency of instruction.

If interrupters are not used, a student can be disengaged from active learning for as many as 75 minutes of a 90-minute class. Even if a student is the person "wearing the most blue" and must awake from a stupor to pick up something for the team, that student must get up and move, a good first step to rejoining the class intellectually. As you think of good interrupters, keep in mind that **movement with a purpose** is a wonderful principle to invoke. In addition, use structures that require noise and/or physical contact between classmates. It is more difficult to sleep when your partner is poking you and asking you questions, demanding a response.

Creating effective interrupters and knowing when to use them are goals for the good teacher. One of these is called **Pairs Ask Quickly** and is described below.

Pairs Ask Quickly (Ask your partner FIRST)

Near the beginning of a presentation or lecture the listeners are processing material at a high rate, but as time passes, the quality of the reception of material declines. If there is not a change in the manner of presentation, the level at which learning is occurring can continue to deteriorate. One quick fix which causes people to reflect on what has been shared is to train the audience to do effective **Pairs Ask Quickly**.

Ask each member in the group of listeners to select a partner from the team—a team which has been carefully selected and built by you. A **visual response** such as giving your partner a "high five" gives assurance that the pairing has occurred. Share with the pairs that at certain times in the lecture a question will be stated for each person to consider. When an agreed upon cue is given, the partners will quickly ask each other the question. No talking should have happened until the cue is presented. The partner that is first to repeat the complete question becomes the listener and the other partner, who was slower to repeat the question, must give the partner an answer to the question. Soon both partners are discussing the question, and the discussion between the partners deepens. Consensus is possible although not an essential goal. A time cue is presented indicating the amount of time left to discuss. It can be a message like "30 seconds left" written and displayed on an erase-and-wipe board. Several pairs can be asked to share the content of their discussion with the group. After this brief interlude, the presentation or lecture continues. The result is often an increase in the listening efficiency.

For practice, an initial question could be something simple like:

Ask your partner:

> Where were you born?
>
> What is the date today?
>
> What are you doing this weekend?
>
> What is your favorite color?
>
> What is the last book you read?

I have found that when using Pairs Ask Quickly a question like the following motivates the students. Suppose I was teaching a group about Think/Pair/Square/Share and wanted them to reflect upon this strategy. I would say to the class that when the cue was supplied each person had to say these words as quickly as possible, "Oh partner. What do you think is the advantage of asking key questions using **Think/Pair/Square/Share**?" And I would tell them that it was imperative that they say "Oh partner" first. I would repeat the question to be asked, say something like "Ready, set" and then supply the cue and listen to the class race to win the contest. Much laughter fills the classroom and the "losing" partners respond to the question. Soon all the kids are talking and students who had drifted away are engaged once more.

This strategy could be used after the initial segment of a lesson. Soon after the presentation has begun the partners could be asked to think about the subject of today's lesson without speaking. After a moment, provide the **Pairs Ask Quickly** cue as the nature of the presentation is considered by the partners. When appropriate, during the body of the presentation, stop at key points to have the partners ask and discuss what has been said or consider a developmental question motivating a topic yet to be presented, beginning the question with, "Oh Partner."

At the close of a presentation or a class use **Pairs Ask Quickly** to summarize the lesson. Simply ask the pairs to become quiet and perhaps ask, "Oh partner, what did we learn today?" On cue, they each attempt to be first to ask the question of the partner. What generally happens is that both partners participate fully in the discussion. Learning should be enjoyable, even fun, and the students seem to have a great time using the **Pairs Ask Quickly** structure.

In some classes, planned pairing may be advisable to improve the sharing. My experience has been that when **Pairs Ask Quickly** is used, students are on task more continuously during a class period, anticipating the cue to ask a partner question, but not knowing when it will be given. The discussion between the partners tends to deepen the learning. If time is provided for select pairs to share the results of their discussion, unanticipated perspectives enrich the subject matter.

Educational Interrupters keep students "plugged in" and we teachers need to be creative in generating more of them. No wonder I love this teaching so very much; it keeps you thinking. You do not just stand and talk at a group of kids. You are always being presented with challenges that energize and excite.

Going Beyond the Curriculum

The opportunities to positively impact young people's lives are treasured events and add substance to the teaching career. During class discussions, meaningful life truths can be shared. Sometimes years later students will write and thank you for teaching them life skills like always being a NGU, a never-give-upper. A truth like that is reinforced as the teacher models that trait throughout the year. I have taken time each summer to make a list of truths I would intentionally teach my students the following year. These truths would be part of my class syllabus as well as visibly observed in my life. How valuable it is to teach these qualities on purpose! Long after students have forgotten the quadratic formula, which my students would stand up and sing like a math chorus, I hope they remember to practice empathy, to encourage, to comfort and to come alongside and help another person. These behaviors can be so powerfully taught and practiced in a collaborative classroom. My observation has been that as a group of students increasingly demonstrates these qualities, the class performance on academic skills improves as well. The choice is *not* to teach these affective skills *or* the academic ones but to teach *both together*. In addition, as I will look back on my life, I will know that it has been substantial if both types of skills have been taught to my students.

The reason I believe this about teaching is that I experienced it in my own life. Coaching is teaching, and my own high school basketball coach, John Czycasi, taught all of his players good basketball skills; however, what he taught us about life has remained with me and continues to be a valuable part of my life. While coaching our team, Cy taught me that working hard toward a goal was a quality that real men displayed. He also showed us that we could be intense with each other toward achieving that goal and be friends and teammates whether we won or lost. He demanded that we respect our own players as well as the opposing team, thereby teaching us to do so. He exhibited a deep concern for his players even when we lost the state championship. He valued us more than our accomplishments. I occasionally drop in to see him just to express my thanks for the vital part he played in my own personal growth.

Whether I am teaching a class, helping to coach a team or tutoring an individual student, my hope and desire is to have a positive impact on the lives of my students. We teachers are totally blessed to be called to teach!

The Baseline for the Class

Some years ago, after nine years of marriage, my wife and I were blessed with the expectation of our first child. We had excitedly anticipated the arrival of this young one; however, early problems resulted in my wife being restricted to bed rest starting in the third month of pregnancy. The baby was born after seven months, weighing 2 pounds 15 ounces and having serious health problems. We were now told that there was a good chance that the young baby might not last the week. We were encouraged to enjoy our baby who was lying on a steel table attached to a respirator and other equipment as he fought for precious life, which was seriously threatened by hyaline membrane disease. Priscilla and I were almost afraid to love this child that we might lose, yet love him we did. My wife almost never left our baby's side. I had to teach middle school each day, driving the hour's journey to the hospital at the end of the school day. (There was no maternity leave for men in those days.)

At the close of the first weekend the miracle of life was still there in our baby and he was placed in an isolette. He had graduated, but still was in danger. We were so grateful for the continuation of his young life. Two weeks after our son's birth I received a fateful call at school saying that, "Your baby has gone bad." Those words left me in a state of helpless fear. I raced to the hospital and joined my wife as we prayed and cried until there were no more tears. During this time, my wife had created a colorfully decorated card that she fixed to the isolette. The card contained the words, "I am fearfully and wonderfully made." Every finger and every toe, no matter how small, were works of art, parts of the miracle that was our child. We spent a fitful night, but in the morning that little heart was still beating. As I drove back home, after doing my lesson plans in the hospital hallway, I began thinking about my middle school students. Each of them was also fearfully and wonderfully made just like my son. How do I tell them? I remembered as a math major proving that solutions were unique and how that made those solutions truly special. I decided that I would tell each one of them that he or she was "**Unique and Valuable**."

I remember little Sammy coming to my low-skills math class the next day, a young boy with an unfortunate home life. He often wore soiled clothes and lived in an unkempt trailer, which I had visited. Abuse of alcohol was a major part of his parents' lives. As he came into class that day I shook his small hand and I said, "Sammy, you are unique and valuable." So it went as each child entered that day. Of course, I had to explain the meanings of those words, but the person most profoundly affected by this was me as I had found a way to describe how I truly felt about each child that I taught.

Near the beginning of each year, I share these same words with each class that I teach. I ask the kids to go to **Think Mode** and write five meanings or uses for the word *unique*. A wonderful strategy for getting feedback from a group is to use **Circle of Knowledge**. One person in each group reads to the team one meaning of the word *unique*. Everyone in the group checks their own list. If the meaning read is on the list, a check is put next to that meaning. If the meaning read is not on the list, that meaning is added to the bottom of the list. The next person in the group reads a meaning and the same process is followed around the "circle" of the team. This continues until each person has said "pass," meaning my list has been exhausted. If this is done correctly, then each person in a group has the same list as the other members of the group, although in a different order. Then I conduct **Circle of Knowledge** in the classroom, following the procedure described above; this time each team supplies one meaning of the word *unique* and everyone checks the list, adding meanings when necessary.

Suppose that I had the only Mickey Mantle rookie card in existence in the world. That card would certainly be unique. What else would it be? It would be valuable and I would be wealthy and I certainly would not have that card here in this class without an armed guard. The card would be encased in some protective shield. The students are told that just like that baseball card everyone in this class is unique and valuable, a treasure and deserving of respect.

Using one of the student's list I read to the class that each of them is rare, a treasure, one of a kind, original, an individual, special, and so on. Each student gives a partner a "High 5" and tells that person that, "You are unique and valuable." In turn, each member of a team tells each other member of the team the same thing. Unique and valuable things are treated in special ways. Unique and valuable people need to **act** in special ways. They do not take illegal drugs, do not treat one another as possessions, do show empathy to others, do encourage and help others, do homework every night and do treat everyone in a respectful way. We all agree that each of us is unique and valuable and that in this class we will *act* unique and valuable.

This philosophy becomes the baseline of the class for the year. It softens the competition. When a team loses the championship, they can still join hands and declare, "We may have lost, but we are still unique and valuable." A student who has acted inappropriately toward another student can be asked, "Did you treat that person as unique and valuable?" The students are regularly reminded of this philosophy.

I would offer one caution—never tell a class that they are unique and valuable unless you are committed to treating each student as unique and valuable in all situations, even when a student tells you to do something to yourself that is biologically impossible. Students quickly recognize hypocrisy and we teachers need to believe what we tell kids and practice it in front of them.

Along with this, students need to hear that, *"Choices have consequences; therefore, make wise choices."* The teacher makes sure the students know the consequences for negative behaviors and is committed to applying those consequences where appropriate, but doing so without anger.

These two foundational philosophies are reinforced each day. Sometimes I repeat them and other times I have the students repeat them. When I had the privilege of teaching in the same room all day, three bulletin boards were designated to communicate these truths, visibly displaying them as the students entered the room. We always attempt to treat each other as unique and valuable. On the final exam the last question is a True/False question asking, "Are you unique and valuable?" The only possible answer is "True."

Students communicate to me that the "Unique and Valuable" philosophy has had a profound impact on their lives. Many have said, "No one ever told me I was unique and valuable before." It is a philosophy that will be remembered long after much of the mathematics has been forgotten. Former students I have not seen in many years will greet me with, "I am still unique and valuable. Are you?" The exact words are not crucial, but the concept of the worth and value of each student is vital. With this as a practiced philosophy, many good things can occur in a classroom.

Incidentally, the inspiration for this philosophy, the birth of our baby in difficult times, had a wonderful outcome. After 50 days in the neo-natal intensive care nursery, he was joyfully brought home. He is truly unique and valuable as are my daughter and wife and, for that matter, everyone that I teach and each person I meet. Viewing others this way genuinely enriches teaching, family and life. Teaching students to view others this way gives another dimension of worth to the time spent with our students.

I always remind the students that the teacher is also unique and valuable and should be treated that way as well. Once this philosophy is firmly established, the classroom becomes a family or team and a sense of freedom prevails among us. For me, it makes the classroom an absolutely joyful place in which to work.

Establishing this philosophy allows us to solve most problems internally, leaving the school administration time to deal with more important matters. Every classroom experiences conflict and when it does occur I can take the participants aside and remind them of the uniqueness and value of themselves and of the other person. Usually, the kids admit they had forgotten and treated the other person as common and worthless. Apologies are offered and class continues, often with the two offenders cooperating at a high level.

The uniqueness of each student is highlighted when a student transfers to another school leaving behind memories of that student stirred by the sight of an empty desk. Losing all my students at the end of the school year is tough, but having one unexpectedly leave during the year is especially difficult, creating a void which cannot be filled. I feel as if I have been robbed of precious moments.

During my first years of teaching in a big city school I discovered that I was unprepared for the most excruciating loss, when one of my students was taken from me due to an act of violence. One instance of this was especially painful. I was privileged to coach a group of young men as they played in competitive basketball tournaments. One year the kids had great success, qualifying for a week-long national tournament in New York. The team won a regional tournament on a Saturday night allowing us to receive the national invitation. Leading the team to victory was Tommy, an All-American high school player. As I entered my inner-city high school on Monday morning, my team manager met me with the words I will never forget, "Tommy's gone away from here." He meant that Tommy had died on Sunday as a result of a violent confrontation with another young person, an act in which Tommy was wrongfully assaulted. The other young men and I discussed, questioned and struggled with many things, especially our own mortality as well as for what purpose we each would live our lives. It was a painful time that resulted in our growing together. Robert replaced Tommy on the team, and we dedicated the national championship to Tommy.

Tommy's uniqueness and value was brought home to me as I carried his neatly folded, clean team uniform back to its place of storage. I looked at the empty jersey, realizing how much would not be experienced by Tommy and how the world would be diminished because of his early death.

Every student is unique and valuable.

What a privilege! What a calling it is to teach!

In the Appendix are copies of the class baseline which can be reproduced and given to students to be placed in their notebooks. We all need to remember these very important truths.

Teaching to Learn

I had the privilege of teaching a young Vietnamese girl in an algebra class. She spoke almost no English, but her math skills were outstanding and she soon became the hero of her learning team leading them to several championships. I used communication cards with her, the cards containing important words and phrases in English and Vietnamese. By the time she was a senior, she had become quite proficient in English. She said that our class in algebra had reminded her of her father's sayings. Only now could she tell me about that. Her father, still a farmer in Vietnam, had told her, "It is not your skill until you have taught another person how to do it." Teaching a concept is a great way to truly master that concept.

Many years ago I was asked to teach an advanced mathematics course which would occur after the normal school day. Two students from high schools in our county had completed 2 years of advanced placement calculus prior to their senior year of high school. I accepted the opportunity to teach them differential equations, including many topics in linear algebra. At first, my inclination was to decline, but when I was told I would be paid and I knew those earnings would allow me to do things during my summer other than landscaping and painting houses, I accepted. No longer would I need to look for jobs to supplement my teaching income. Bring it on!

After accepting the offer in June, I began studying by looking at my old college notes and tests. Much of the material I still remembered. It was when I began to write lesson plans that the struggle began. I knew enough to do well on my college tests, but I did not have the necessary mastery to teach another person the material, especially when you consider that I would be the least capable person in the classroom. The amount of effort and time I invested was significant. Despite the struggle, the more I taught the course, the more skilled I became with the material. Teaching proved to be an effective way to learn, and the two students also had a good learning experience.

How could I put this philosophy to work in my classroom? I created the Player/Coach activity to encourage students to teach each other. It has been used with wonderful results in classrooms of many grades, subjects and levels. Player/Coach is similar to Kagan's Pairs Check activity.

Player/Coach

In a classroom of 34 students and 1 teacher, there are often 35 teachers because, at certain times, every student can be a teacher. Often, teachers have indicated that a particular subject was learned best when the learner was required to teach the subject. My experience has reinforced this truth that teaching has a double effect; the learner learns and the teacher learns. Teaching is truly an activity that can be classified as "double arrowed." I teach and I learn. I teach and you learn. The player/coach activity allows the students to experience the value of teaching to learn as well as the benefits of interacting with a peer.

The player/coach structure should be modeled for the entire class by the teacher and a selected student. With the entire class observing, first the teacher becomes the coach and then the student plays the coach's role. The skill to be taught should be fairly familiar to the entire class with a deepening of that skill yet to be accomplished. The coach role requires that person to take the lead in the pair. The coach first encourages the player to do well and assures the player that learning will occur. The coach begins to address the question or the problem, either by demonstration or by asking a leading question of the player. Suppose the skill is to solve linear equations like $2x + 3 = 15$. The coach might ask, "How do we begin?" or "What is our final goal?" Depending on the player's answer, the coach takes more or less of a lead in reaching a conclusion.

If the player is very uninformed about this skill, the coach does more of the problem, speaking aloud, describing each step of the analysis. This should be a noisy activity, and this is good, purposeful noise. Structured noise can be a sign of much learning. The coach should check for understanding by asking the player if each step is clear. If the player seems to understand, the coach can be more of a guide, working the problem at the direction of the player. The coach is the only one actually writing; the player is observing, questioning and/or directing. The coach should ask the player to describe out loud what has just been done. At the conclusion of the work, the player should thank the coach, perhaps shaking hands.

Now, the roles are switched and the former player becomes the coach, the one who will write, and the former coach becomes the player. Sometimes several sets of this activity are profitable and at other times letting each partner assume each role once is sufficient. Generally, the majority of the class is on task and much learning occurs.

During the activity, the classroom teacher roams, being sensitive to the varying needs of the class. For the initial activity, the classroom teacher can select the first coach by determining which of the partners seems to have a better understanding of the skill.

Some new strategies create an educational need and player/coach did that for me. I saw the advantages of having all my players and coaches in pairs at the blackboard, but I did not have enough board space for 30 pairs of students. After explaining the benefits of this idea to my principal, he arranged for extra chalk boards to be constructed in my classroom. Having a principal for whom instruction was a top priority was indeed a blessing!

Later as a floater, I taught in some rooms with limited board space so I would send half the class in their pairs to the board while the other half worked in pairs at their desks. The two groups of students would switch locations at some point during the activity. Changing position and the resulting movement allowed for students to freshly engage in learning.

The coach activities are to encourage, assure, demonstrate, guide, speak the steps aloud and write down the conclusions. The player observes, asks questions, speaks back the coach's words and thanks the coach.

Student Enforcers

Some classes can present genuine control and management challenges that drain the energy and time of a teacher and result in a diminished learning environment. The teacher can put much energy into getting the students to pay attention and cooperate, energy that could be spent better in learning activities.

In this situation I choose one person from each team to be a team enforcer, someone who is assertive and reasonably on task most of the time. If this person is empathetic, that will also be an asset. While the class is socializing—a balanced amount of social interaction is healthy, just like in the workplace—or working on an activity, I meet with the students who will become my first enforcers or sheriffs. I explain that they are essential to the quality of the learning in this classroom. I tell them that I will provide a cue and they will supply a response that will result in the class becoming quiet. Up until this point I had been using the ringing of a hand-held bell to get the students to quiet down. The enforcers will be expected to teach everyone in the team both the cue and the response so that when I give the cue, every student in the class will be giving the response.

The cue will be my voice saying "Enforcers, three" while I hold up three fingers. At that moment the enforcers will lead the group with the response, which is making a "Shhh" sound with their lips and extending both arms with palms out. Every person in the class should be offering the response. We try the cueing and response several times asking the enforcers to reteach some of the teams. I will make it competitive, saying that the next time I present the cue, the team with the best response will be rewarded with team competition points, or whatever reward is appropriate.

The students say "Goodbye" to the bell and they assume their role in classroom management. The enforcer/sheriffs are given the role cards found in the appendix. After 5 class periods another person becomes the team enforcer. This continues until each person has been the enforcer after which the enforcer role is put on the shelf. Everyone in the class has been trained to be the enforcer and in June on a hot day after a fight has occurred in the hall and the kids are flying high, all I have to do is to supply the cue and some of the natural enforcers in the class initiate the response, resulting in a quiet class. It is truly not my class, but it is *our* class. The teacher and the students manage the class.

New Schedules Motivate Teachers to Create and Improve

How things have changed with respect to school schedules! In the past it seemed that everyone was on the same one or two schedules, the 6-period day or the 7-period day. Now there seems to be a schedule to fit any situation. In the past 20 years, I have experienced 4 different schedules. Each schedule has unique advantages and disadvantages, resulting from the particular characteristics each embodies. Adjusting to a new schedule demands some creativity, which is not a bad thing for a teacher who desires to keep the classroom refreshing and efficient.

Among the many adjustments to be made, one involved the curriculum being taught. Our school changed from a 6-period day to an alternating block schedule with one period meeting for 48 minutes each day for the entire school year. Computations revealed that in going to the new block schedule the actual instructional time would be reduced by 1350 minutes. Even after gaining increased efficiency with the block, this reduction in time would not allow for teaching the entire Algebra II curriculum that our county had established. After 2 weeks in the new schedule, I realized some changes had to occur. The first was to rein in the major time waster in the classroom—namely, me, the teacher. I purchased and began to use a timer. It became my guide, not my god, keeping me on track. I wish I had used one back in the previous schedule with the extra 1350 minutes. The administrative powers in the county did not anticipate the curriculum crunch and made no changes, leaving the teacher in a tough situation.

I decided someone needed to do something and so I created a new curriculum. To do this, I gave the teachers of pre-calculus a content outline of the Algebra II curriculum and asked them to highlight the foundational topics they wanted students to know. I included the skills important for high stakes testing and I put in the curriculum topics I knew were vital and beautiful. I made a decision to establish 5 strands, each strand composed of related topics. As each strand was taught, one topic led to another topic naturally. We might begin on page 1 in the book, moving to page 35, then to 125 and so on until we might finish the strand on page 543. Then a new strand would begin, perhaps on page 42. The result was a course loved by the students and the teacher. Other teachers adopted this "new" curriculum and used it for several years until our school system made the changes that fit the block. The cart gets in front of the horse sometimes and that makes the cart driver think and create.

Other adjustments to the block schedule involve teaching strategies. When I was following an alternating day schedule where we used an "A" day and a "B" day, a special set of circumstances required a new strategy.

Let's say I had scheduled a test for Friday, a "B" day and school was cancelled due to inclement weather. On our system Monday was an "A" day. A dance assembly was scheduled for Tuesday, the next "B" day, and although the performers were excellent and the assembly enjoyable, my students would be taking the test on Thursday, the next "B" day 8 days after I had last seen these students a week ago Wednesday. In spite of the fact that all my students used these extra days to better prepare for the test, I felt constrained to create a structure that would help them to be more ready for the exam, an activity which would create a good mind-set to do their best. It is called **Pairs Rehearsal** as described earlier in the book. The students using their notebooks, information sheets supplied by the teacher or some other resource were better able to have success even when the class had not met for a number of days.

Teaching in a block schedule has caused me to create and refresh my teaching style and kept me from becoming stagnant. I am thankful for the differences the block schedule has made in my teaching.

PRINCIPLES FOR CREATING AN ENGAGING CLASSROOM

DEVELOP/DEEPEN RELATIONSHIPS OF STUDENTS WITH EACH OTHER AND BETWEEN STUDENTS AND TEACHER.

PRESENT MATERIAL IN VARIOUS WAYS.

MAKE POSITIVE USE OF EDUCATIONAL INTERRUPTERS.

CREATE AN ATMOSPHERE WHERE STUDENTS ENGAGE WITH OTHER STUDENTS ABOUT THE SUBJECT MATERIAL.

FIND WAYS FOR STUDENTS TO MOVE PRODUCTIVELY DURING THE CLASS PERIOD.

CREATE A FAMILY OF LEARNERS.

USE EVERY MINUTE/NO DOWN TIME.

STUDENTS ARE ALWAYS ACCOUNTABLE TO SOMEONE.

Chapter 8

Student Feedback/Advice

What Students Say About Cooperative Learning

The day I decided to create a cooperative environment in my classroom was the beginning of a new career for me. I had taught for 12 years using the traditional recitation model to instruct. I believe I was an effective, entertaining lecturer, but something was missing. Once students began to engage each other in discussions about the class material I realized how much more was gained. Lecture is still an important teacher activity, but it is not the only useful strategy. Lecture is made interactive by addressing key questions using the Think/Pair/Square/Share strategy.

One of the effects of adopting a way of instruction that emphasized students working in teams was the lowering of my stress level. The students take on increased responsibility for the learning and the class management. The teacher has more freedom to mingle with the students and give extra time to teams of students who are struggling. Another positive effect for me and others who have made the same choice is a refreshing renewal. Much of the renewal you can experience will depend on your willingness to **adapt** anything you borrow from others; the need to adapt requires you to **create**; the experience of creating for the classroom gives you **renewed energy and enthusiasm**. My last 26 years of teaching have been exciting and fun and this is related to a changed approach to the classroom.

Students have expressed similar feelings independent of the type or level of the class. Reading the following unedited feedback from three classes of Algebra I Part A provides a small picture of how kids feel about a collaborative classroom.

The following question was asked of three Algebra 1A classes at Mt. Hebron High School in June after a year in a collaborative classroom:

"What do you like about cooperative learning?"
All of the responses are listed below (unedited):

You don't have to be silent the whole period.

I like the fact that if I need help in class I can ask a partner without interrupting you.

I think it was fun by competing for pops.

The fact that your fellow students are able to learn from their own classmates what they don't understand and vice versa.

You may seek help within your group where you may talk freely.

I like being able to learn from different people. I think cooperative learning is more interesting.

You can get better individual attention.

You get different perspectives on how to do a certain type of problem—you get taught different ways.

We try hard to learn because of the teams' competition.

First of all it is very fun. You are always trying your best. It's like baseball if you try your hardest work with your teamates you will win the pennant. In class you will win lollipops if you do the same thing.

I think it helps people to learn easy.

I think being able to help each other.

That you can get help from another student. Everyone can learn something together and have their own group opinions.

It's easier to learn. It helps the stundents to teach each other and gives the teacher a breaks and you are able to make new friends and change your image. I really liked it.

If you don't understand something and the teacher is busy helping another student you can ask one of your group members and they help you learn it as well as a teacher could.

I like it when your not sure how to do something you have your friends to help you and not only your teacher.

You get to see what people are like and meet new friends and also get to help people and kind of show off your smarts.

It gives students a chance to teach students.

A student gets a chance to be taught by not only the teacher, but other classmates, which seems to me a better chance at learning.

Cooperative learning makes our work fun. You can make great friends while learning.

I like to get team points for the quizzes. Its a lot of fun.

It is a good experience to work with other people and you get closer to your classmates. Most of all you and your partners learn as a unit.

You can talk to people in your group.

You learn more and if your teacher can't help you your teammates can.

It gets people involved in helping other people in getting better grades.

It's a fun and exciting way to learn. It's not boring. It's not a dull routine and it's fun to compete against other teams sometimes you *can* learn more from fellow students.

It was fun being in groups and working with fellow classmates.

Well, I liked getting to know people better and it makes learning a lot of fun.

If you don't understand a certain problem this kind of learning helps you because everyone works together to get things done easily and right.

I can learn more from a friend rather than a teacher.

Make new friends and get along better with your classmates.

I like learning as a team.

It's easier to learn. It's fun. It's not boring.

The togetherness of both student's and teacher's.

It gives us a break in taking notes so that we can get together and understand better.

You learn and understand more.

When the teacher goes too fast it's good to have other people on my team to try and help me to understand because almost always at least one person on the team knows what they're doing.

Well, it seems that people your own age understand why you can't comprehend a certain skill, and they can try to help you with it. It's nice to not feel in the dark about something.

I think its fun! It gives students a chance to work together. It gives students a goal and why to work, for team points, LOLLIES.

I liked being in teams, we learn more and faster. I think we should have cooperative learning in all the classes.

I find I can learn easier from someone my own age.

Kids learn better when other kids teach them because they are on their level and they know the difficulties we can have with our work.

I like having the opportunity to ask for help from a friend.

I like the way kids can help other kids, If someone is afraid of asking a question in class they can ask there team mate with out being imberressed. If you add up all the good points of cooperative learning you can have a great list.

. . . but it's even a greater feeling when you can teach someone and know that your the one who helped em pass!

class never gets boring because you are given the chance to talk to your group and help each other out. And when you feel like you've really helped someone understand something they were lost in it makes ya feel really good about yourself.

Everything.

It should be used in all classes in all schools.

I like changing groups because you got to work with different people and really get to know them.

You learn faster . . . someone in your group can help you one on one.

It's easier and you get to talk.

It gives your friends a chance to teach you.

It gives you a better chance to learn.

In all three algebra classes competitive teams were used as the basic class structure. Of great interest to me was what the students had learned in the affective skills. The following question was asked of the classes:

"What did you learn in this class other than math skills?"
All of the responses are supplied below (unedited).

How to cooperate with other students.

How to teach and learn about students.

Team Work to get pop's.

That you could have fun while learning.

That I am unique, valuable, have a mind and have the right to learn.

How to get along better with people.

How to have more pateents with people.

Chris had a crush on Billy.

Responsibility, Friendship, how to work.

How to be a better person.

That you are unique and valuable.

To never give up.

Not to give "up! That you shouldn't judge people by there appearence. There is more to a person than meets the eye I

I learned how to help people and a lot of people needs help.

Sharing, working with others.

. . . how to be myself.

You learn how to respect people.

To care about someone else. Be responsible for others.

I learned more about my classmates and how they, feel and act.

I learned how to be a real caring and derected person, I learned to do things for other people besides myself.

I learned what cooperative learning was.

That each student has the ability to respect others and help others.

I learned how to help other people and to recieve help from people my own age.

I learned that I am somebody and that I have a mind.

Mostly team work.

To make friends, to respect other people.

Cooperation.

How to get people to listen.

That other people have just as much a right to learn as I do.

How to gwt along with other people beter.

Integrity.

That if you know something that not to keep it to yourself, but to teach someone else.

I learned that each person in the class has weak spots yet very capable in other things.

The world does'nt rotate around me.

All teachers make choices about the classroom environment to be used each year and there are many fine options. Choosing the appropriate structure is vital because we get to have those particular students for just 135 hours or so and we teachers want to leave a positive imprint on their lives. Each year I reread the above responses and each reading causes me to make the same choice—to create a cooperative learning environment using pairs and teams of students.

Advice

Try One Idea That You Believe In

I would like to offer some advice to those teachers who decide to introduce cooperative components into their teaching style. Choose an idea or strategy that you *believe is good for kids*. Do not choose a new strategy just because someone directs you to do it, nor something that is the latest fad or just because it appears in this book. We have many fads in education and today's fads will go out of style and then reappear in 25 years as the newest ideas to save our students. Select something that you are convinced is beneficial for your classroom. By the way, you should also believe that the strategy is good for teachers as well—specifically, good for you.

More than likely, you will fail using the new strategy at first, but because you *believe in it* you will fix it and try it again. Failure may await you again, but you will fix it until it works. This strategy will become yours forever. Additional modifications will certainly be required, but it is yours. When you attempt a new idea that you believe in, you should not quit when experiencing failure. I have found this process to be true for all the important things in my life. For example, I married Priscilla because I loved her and believed that I wanted to spend my entire life with her. Believe it or not, I failed as a husband many times—just ask her—but with Priscilla's help I kept fixing it and now she tells me that I am a very good husband. It was the same with being a father. I became a father because I believed it was something we needed and wanted to experience, a desire that grew out of a deepening love we shared. My kids would be most glad to tell you of my many failures, some of which still provide us with laughs and entertainment today. Again, with my family's help I fixed my mistakes and now am described as an excellent father. I won't even tell you about my golf game, but it follows the same set of principles.

If you do things because you believe in them, you will modify and adjust them, but you will never quit.

Make Changes Gradually

Let me remind you that you already do wonderful things in your classroom, and if anything I have written here seems like a good idea, just fit one or two ideas into what you already are doing. Change slowly, making sure you can become excellent at the new strategies you are implementing. Do not attempt too much too fast. Think about who you will be as a teacher in 5 or 10 years. If each year you use just one or two new interactive ideas, after 5 years your classroom will be radically changed. In 10 years you will have forgotten how you used to teach. I know this happened to me. Should you try too much too quickly you may decide that this approach to teaching just does not work and simply bag it. *Go slowly.* Become skilled at each new concept. *Adapt* the ideas to fit you, your kids, your furniture, your school and its specific characteristics.

Now there are some of you that I call the "super sponges," the people who can soak up a bunch at once and can introduce many new ideas with much success. I wish I could be like you. I greatly admire you. The key here is that you know, and only you know, what is the appropriate amount of change for you to make in a certain amount of time. Be yourself and don't try to be someone else. Make the right amount of change for you.

The best cooperative learning strategy for your collaborative classroom has not yet been created. You are the expert who will invent it.

Five Components of Cooperation

When you do generate that new cooperative idea try to give attention to each of the following components (Johnson, Johnson, & Holubec, 1993):

Team Goals

Team members need to know what the objective is for the team. The goal could be to have the highest team average on a quiz, or to be the team that improved the most from their last performance, or to achieve an agreed upon minimum score on a quiz, or to complete a team project.

Make sure that there is a goal and that each team is clear about the specifics of the goal. Of course, the ultimate goal is for each team member to learn.

Team Interaction

Create an environment which encourages students to talk to each other, to check each other's work, to defend and discuss concepts, to help each other review and to make collaborative decisions.

Positive Interdependence

This is best understood by the statement that "We sink or we swim together." Use structures that value the learning and performance of every person on the team. A team should find it very difficult to win or to have success unless each person on the team learns and achieves.

Social Skills

When students are pulled out of the rows and placed in groups where interaction is encouraged, the use of social skills will increase. Know in advance that social skills will need to be modeled and taught. All students, some more than others, will need to develop the necessary interpersonal skills. In the secondary school this is mostly done by the teacher reacting to the behaviors of the students, praising the use of positive skills and teaching a better behavior to a student who has not acted appropriately. Where time permits, a related role-play activity can be used to demonstrate a desired behavior.

Individual Accountability

In order to be sure that each student learns, make sparing use of group quizzes or graded team projects. Measure the contribution of each person. If this is not done, students will reduce the quality and amount of cooperation, letting the more capable or more willing student do all the work. The team will score high, but individual students may learn little, and both students and parents will justifiably complain.

You are the person who knows your class and yourself the best. With these 5 components in mind, go ahead and create the classroom that will result in joyful, effective learners.

In the next chapter you will read about Carolina Pairs and Teams, a cooperative learning structure that I created to fit my needs. Carolina includes the five components described above.

Peer Coaching

Often it is the practice of people who work out with weights to do so in pairs. The partners provide safety when the muscles fail and the weight could become harmful. The pairs encourage each other when the routine becomes tedious and difficult. The two help each other with suggestions about technique and limits. I would suggest that attempting a new strategy in a classroom is much like starting a new workout routine with weights and having a teacher partner could prove invaluable. If you have decided to institute Think/Pair/Team/Share for key questions in your classroom, having a partner who is also trying this for the first time or someone who is a veteran with this structure could be a great help. Perhaps you could arrange for visits to each other's classroom to observe, learn and advise. Having such a partner could make the difference between success and failure.

When choosing a cooperative partner, choose someone with whom you can mutually share in this learning experience. The person may be in your field of teaching, but this is not necessary. Yes, even a math person and a history person can work profitably together. What is important is that each of you believes that the strategy you are going to use is good for kids and teachers and that your pairing will result in *both* of you becoming better at your calling.

Chapter 9

Carolina Pairs/ Carolina Teams

Carolina Pairs and Teams

Have you ever taught that "class from hell?" I had a class where all the cooperative learning in the world had not made a difference and we were struggling. We did a Think/Pair/Square/Share on what was wrong with this class. Finally, one young man asked me why I never gave the members of a team extra points on their quiz grades when they cooperated well. Hey, I am one of those rigorous, heartless math teachers. Points for cooperation—you've got to be kidding! Instead of expressing my true feelings about that idea I actually demonstrated some wisdom and said that I would think about it. I would have time to think on my four-hour drive to Virginia to conduct a workshop for teachers. How ironic that the teacher who had no solutions for this class would be teaching other teachers about teaching!

From that trip, conducting the workshop, discussion with a teacher of English and the drive home came a strategy which answered the young man's question and became a good answer for creating successful learning environments for the next 18 years.

When I presented the idea of Carolina Pairs to that troubled class, they enthusiastically expressed their approval, saying that finally they would receive tangible rewards in exchange for their excellent behavior.

The following quote represents the goal I have for my classes as we learn to work together.

> "Two are better than one because they have
> a good return on their labor.
> For, if either of them falls, the one will
> lift up his companion.
> But woe to the one who falls when there is not
> Another to lift him up."
>
> Ecclesiastes 4:9,10

The Carolina Pairs and Teams structures are empowered by the content of the above quote. Using Robert Slavin's Student Teams Achievement Division (STAD) structure (Slavin, 1995) was foundational for my creation of Carolina. (Note that I came up with the name because of where I live, but you can feel free to change the name as you use this technique.)

Using Carolina Pairs and Teams

Would you engage in a golf match against Tiger Woods with $10,000 being awarded to the winner? For some it would be a bargain to be able to spend a morning playing golf with Tiger; however, most of us just could not afford the cost. I might be tempted if Tiger would give me a stroke for each hole as well as 4 additional strokes on each of 9 holes for trouble I most certainly would encounter. That would be 22 strokes, meaning if I could score within 21 strokes of Tiger's score, I would win. I might still lose, but at least I could be competitive. If I were required to compete with Tiger for $10,000 over and over again without the stroke adjustment, I would repeatedly lose and eventually become broke and discouraged because I would truly have no chance to be victorious.

Many students feel discouraged because they have very little chance to win, with winning often defined as scoring an "A" on a quiz. Try to imagine yourself as a student in a class where you have been assigned a partner who is also a student in the class. You and your partner will participate in the same learning activities to learn new concepts. The learning activities are the same as those with which you were familiar in the past: a teacher presenting a lesson, independent research, a cooperative learning structure, individual testing, individual study, a laboratory activity or whatever is appropriate. The teacher then gives you time to study with your partner, encouraging you to study outside of class, perhaps exchanging phone numbers and e-mail addresses with your partner, enabling increased communication. You are informed that the class will be evaluated by a quiz or other testing device and that each student will take the quiz independently, without the help of study notes or other students, not even your own partner.

That is not really any different than your past learning experience except for the fact that you have a study partner. The primary difference will be that your grade on the quiz, the grade that is recorded in the teacher's grade book, can be improved by you and your partner's effective cooperation, which will be measured by your improvement *as a pair* over your past quiz performance record. If your total score as a pair improves, then you both will receive *bonus points* added on to your earned grade.

You and your partner can have a very real impact on each other's final grade. What an incentive not only to do well yourself, but also to be sure that your partner does well! It is as if you and your partner form a small company that produces excellence, and earnings are based on the positive effect you have had upon each other during the learning process. *If you are better together than you were apart, then bonus points are given as a reward.*

The bonus point system is quite simple to understand and use. Suppose Sam and Cara are partners in a particular class. *The first task is to determine the pair's initial target score.* Sam's work has been averaging around 82 and Cara's about 92; their combined average is about 87. Their first time target score could be 86, to give them a better opportunity for early success. This is the score they would attempt to equal or to beat. This same score could be handed out to them confidentially on a small square of paper. They will take a quiz obeying individual accountability, which is taking the quiz without the help of anyone else. If their average as a pair is 86 or better, bonus points will be added to their quiz scores *before* they are recorded in the grade book. The number of points which are added as a bonus will vary according to the class and should be carefully determined by the teacher.

Generally the target score should:

a. Reflect the pair's past achievement

b. Be a score which can be reasonably beaten, provided effective partner work is accomplished

c. Supply an appropriate challenge for the pair to work toward and to improve.

An initial target score can be arrived at in any manner deemed fair by the students and the teacher; however a) and b) should be weighted more heavily for the *first time target score.*

In order to preserve the challenge for the pair, nudging them to excellence and to be fair, *the target score for each pair is adjusted after two quizzes or evaluations*: upward if the pair of students has improved, downward if their performance has been disappointing, or no change if their grades have remained relatively constant. The change in target should be made according to the three principles described above. How the teacher weights each of these three will affect the assignment of the new target score. For example, if the pair received bonus on their first quiz but not on the second, then the inclination might be to raise the target in order to motivate the students to stretch a bit or perhaps the old target should be preserved to encourage this pair with additional success opportunities. The teacher makes the decision based upon what will result in an optimum learning experience for the students.

The teacher needs to frequently remind the students about their target score and the impact positive interaction can have on their learning. Often the question should be asked of the students, *"What is the best way to learn more deeply and to improve your grade?"* Of course, the answer is, "By teaching my partner." The receiving of bonus points should be the result of a combined effort of the two partners and not because one person worked and the other "came along for the ride." To safeguard against this, the class could agree that if one of the pair fell below a certain grade or if one of the pair scored more than say 10 points below his or her past average, no bonus points would be given. You may find that neither of these "circuit breakers" is either appropriate or necessary.

When a student is absent on quiz day, the student may take a makeup on the next day, remaining eligible for bonus points. Another *possible* requirement that emphasizes the value of attendance is the forfeiture of the opportunity for "bonus" should one of the pair be absent on quiz day. This can be judged on an individual basis depending on what is appropriate for that specific class. One possible outcome is that students *may* encourage one another to come to school. If chronically absent students have been identified and placed in a Carolina trio, two targets can be used—one when all three students are present on quiz day and one when the student with the high absentee record is missing. In that case only the students in attendance on quiz day are eligible for bonus. The teacher, as the expert educator, will determine what is best for each case.

Suppose we are in a class where Alex and Shayla are students and the number of bonus points added is 3. A record of possible scores for the students is written below:

Target Score for the pair is 84.

	Quiz #1	Pair Average	Grade Recorded
Alex	84		87
		88	BONUS EARNED
Shayla	92		95

Remember, 84 is the pair's target.

	Quiz #2	Pair Average	Grade Recorded
Alex	82		85
		85	BONUS EARNED
Shayla	88		91

Their new target could be 85 or 86.

Sometimes the new target can be computed by finding the average of the old target and the two pair averages and then applying common sense as follows:

$$\frac{84 + 88 + 85}{3} \quad \text{is} \quad 85.6$$

Do not let the target spike up or dip down too quickly.

Let's look at another pair of students whose target score is 92:

	Quiz #1	Pair Average	Grade Recorded
Damon	100		103
		95	BONUS EARNED
Laura	90		93

For Damon who received a score of 103 it is as if he has 3 points in the bank.

	Quiz #2	Pair Average	Grade Recorded
Damon	91		91
		90.5	NO BONUS
Laura	90		90

$$\frac{\text{old target + pair average + second pair average}}{3} \quad \text{is} \quad 92.5$$

The new target might be 92 or 93.

Consider Pam and Susan whose target is 76 and whose two pair averages are 88 and 92, respectively. Although the algorithm supplied earlier indicates a new target score of 85 or 86, a wiser new target might be 81 or 82. The goal is to *nudge* them to excellence.

When assigning new targets, keep in mind the difficulty of the material to be learned during the period of the next two evaluations.

In the case when students have a pair average equal to their target, I award them the bonus points. Any average less than the target results in no bonus earned. *No points are ever lost because of a partner's poor performance.*

If a pair should have two successive evaluations where bonus is not earned, I meet with them to determine what they might do differently as they are challenged by the new material.

Carolina Groups or Teams

An adaptation of this structure can be made to cooperative teams, called Carolina Teams. *Students love teams* with their team names, team building and team identity. The camaraderie and the sense of belonging are vital for students' well being and are tremendous tools for effective learning. Teams may be formed by the teacher, by the students and the teacher, or by the students' choice with limited input from the teacher. Care must be taken to make team formation positive for everyone as well as appropriate for achievement by the class. If the students form their own teams, the use of a team interaction contract is advised. Also, it is best not to use the new teams in class until *everyone* has a team; sometimes the teacher has to be a matchmaker to find a team for a particular student. Once teams are formed, team building experienced and team names created, initial team targets need to be established. The first team target is determined in the same manner as that for Carolina Pairs, a little lower than the quiz and test averages for the members of each team. In this system, the pair becomes a trio or a team of 4 or 5. Remember, teams of 5 allow for placement of students who have demonstrated poor attendance.

In addition to the possibility of earning bonus points for each individual on the team, team competition points can be computed and displayed on a scoreboard in the classroom to promote a healthy, controlled competition between the teams, providing a way to encourage student performance. One practice that has proven effective is to crown a champion or champions after 5 to 10 days of active learning. Team competition points may be earned by team performance in class activities, by good attendance or homework completed, by exhibiting creative thoughts or whatever the teacher thinks is important. Many points are awarded for the demonstration of individual learning after the team has cooperated to learn. The largest number of team competition points is earned by the team performance on an evaluation like a quiz or test where individual accountability is observed.

To determine **team competition points** earned by a team, the following procedure may be followed:

a. Grade each student's quiz or test.

b. Find the team average.

c. Divide the team average by the target.

d. Multiply that number by 100 (use a calculator).

The resulting number indicates what percent of the team target was achieved, revealing how much the team *improved*. On the scoreboard this number is added to the points that the team has already earned. These points do *not* go in the grade book. The students soon learn the following:

A team that *hits its target exactly* earns 100 team competition points.

A team that *beats* its target receives *more than 100* competition points.

A team that *falls short* of its target scores *less than 100* points.

If a class has 6 or more teams, divide the class into two divisions, each of which competes against *only* the teams in its division. One division does not compete against the other division. Two champions are guaranteed, increasing the possibility of a team becoming a champion and providing increased incentive for the class.

Some sample team points results are displayed below:

Team Target	Team Quiz Average	Team Points
82	82	100
85	95	112
91	84	92
90	98	109

Notice: The last computation is 98/90 or 1.0888 and becomes 108.88 when multiplied by 100, rounding to 109.

Team points are accumulated for 5 to 10 days; champions crowned and rewarded; points taken down; and a new competition with the same teams begun. Sometimes putting the team names of the champions into the same division is a good thing, especially if it is done when the students are not in the room. This guarantees a new champion in at least one division during the next competition.

The incentives for Carolina Pairs/Teams are to have students' achievement increase and to give students the opportunity to experience the dynamic of joining with another person to produce excellence in learning. Pre-bonus grades have markedly improved in the classes where the Carolina improvement concept has been used. In addition, students have experienced the reward for not only having learned well, but having taught another person and making a positive difference in that person's learning experience. They have also experienced and learned to respond to the disappointment resulting from their own or a partner's poor performance. The students realize that they can and do have an impact on others' lives. We teachers understand all too well that the first time we really learned many things was when we taught them to someone else. Using Carolina, more students have this same experience. Truly, one does become master of a skill when one teaches that skill to another!

Selection of Pairs and Teams

Generally, the teacher selects the first set of Carolina Pairs or Teams in order to ensure that the teams will be effective in their production of excellence. Students do not always value the qualities in others that would help a team to work well together.

How partners are formed is an important step in establishing a Carolina classroom structure. Usually, those students who are placed together are those who will work most effectively with one another. Since the Carolina process is not generally used until the second quarter of a year, the students have already demonstrated their strengths and needs and have been observed in different groupings, so a teacher has a good idea of who will and will not produce excellent results.

We will use the following designations to illustrate ability as compared with other members of a class and not with the population at large.

H-high ability   A-average ability   L-low ability

For a Carolina Pairs class, I use HA, AA, AL, HH and HL. The one pairing I generally do not use is LL because such a pairing limits academic interaction. To use HL, the correct H and the correct L must be selected, often because they share a common interest such as sports. In any case, prior to an HL creation I sell the idea to each person and ask their permission for such a pairing, making sure each understands their respective responsibilities. The one student will teach the majority of the time and the other student will be taught in most instances; for the one it could be a burden and for the other a humbling experience. Some of the greatest success stories have come from an HL pairing.

For years I have used an HH pairing for a Carolina Pair or an HHHH team formation for a Carolina Team. These high achievers drive each other to be better and better thereby pushing the team target to the top. Such a team often finishes their work prior to the other students, making it possible for them to roam the classroom, experiencing the many benefits of teaching and interacting with their classmates in a learning environment. These students check classmates' work, explain concepts and assist as helpers to the teacher.

Since I change teams every 8 to 10 weeks, the HHHH experience is just one of several experiences for these students. HHHH should not be the only team formation these students have. It was not until I was undergoing a knee operation that I fully realized the wisdom of having occasional HHHH teams. This experience also illustrates how those of us who are called to teach never stop thinking about teaching. When teachers get together socially, what do they do? They talk "shop."

I was lying on the operating table watching the surgical nurse, listening to the anesthesiologist and somewhat aware of the person who would be watching my vital signs on several machines. When my surgeon walked in, I thought, "Which of these four people would I want to be the low achiever?" My response just before losing consciousness was that I hoped this was an HHHH team. Several days later I reflected on the fact that often later in life high achievers work with other high achievers. I thought how beneficial it was to let the high achievers have the HHHH experience as *one* of their team structures in the low-risk setting of school; however, this should *not be their only experience*.

Changing pairs or teams is sometimes necessary when problems arise. This happened less frequently *when I waited to select teams until I knew my students very well and until they had had short-term cooperative experiences with a variety of students*. Perhaps an occasional student will not be ready to work profitably with another student due to a lack of appropriate behavior. I will converse with the student privately, often saying that a period of probation will begin, hoping the student will alter the inappropriate behavior. If the situation does not improve, I might ask the student for input about another group placement. Sometimes making a change to a new pair or group resolves the issue. I make changes slowly, always asking the destination group if the change would be positive. Occasionally, for many reasons, nothing works or the student does not desire to be in any group. I am committed to the student having a partner so I share the fact that I will be the student's partner and a new desk will be set aside in a convenient location. In this arrangement, the student is not eligible for bonus points. *It is important that this is a result of choices made by the student*. Sometimes students reconsider their choices and often after a period of time, a student will ask to rejoin the Carolina structure.

The longer that the Carolina system is used the more proficient the teacher will become at pair and team formation until few if any changes are required. First, it is vital for the teacher to become convinced that this is good for kids and then perseverance and patience will result in effective team selection.

Some classes achieve high levels of cooperation resulting in outstanding achievement. When a group of students has done this, they have *earned the right* to have significant input in the selection of their next Carolina Pair or Team. One method allows *both the student and the teacher* to share in the team selection. To do this, each student is given a piece of paper and instructed to place his or her name in an oval in the center of the paper. Then each student is encouraged to write the names of 4 or 5 students with whom effective teamwork might be accomplished. The papers are collected and after class the teacher lays all the papers out on a flat surface and attempts to *make each student happy at least once*. In this manner, obviously poor selections can be avoided while good choices can be rewarded. (See the sample ovals on the next page.) Once in a great while, a student will not be able to be placed with any of the selections on the oval. In that case, place the student with one or more students who selected him or her and inform that student of their request.

At least once each year, a class earns the right to have even more freedom in the team selection. This would be a class of students who exceeded all positive expectations. Each student is given a contract and directed to select their partner or teammates and sign the contract agreeing to specific behaviors. A target date is selected for all contracts to be completed. While this is going on, students are still seated in their old teams or pairs. An occasional student will not turn in a contract, requiring the teacher to become a matchmaker. Only when every student has a team assignment should the new team seating be used. (Sample contracts are provided on the following pages.)

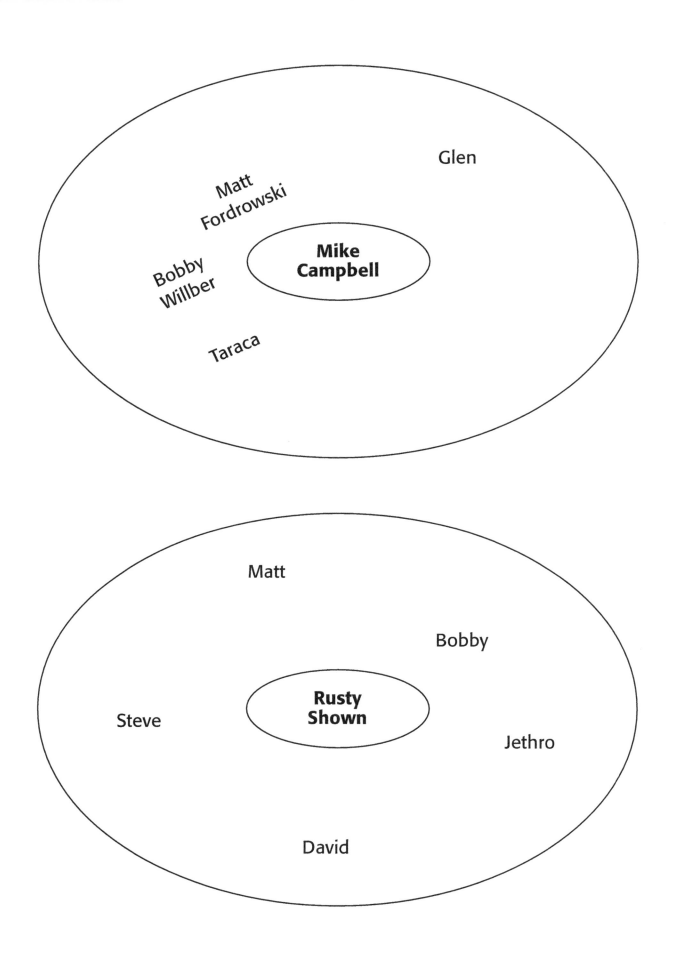

CAROLINA PAIRS

WE AGREE TO HELP EACH OTHER TO HAVE MAXIMUM SUCCESS BY LISTENING PATIENTLY TO ONE ANOTHER'S QUESTIONS, BY ASKING EACH OTHER FOR HELP, BY ASKING IF SOMEONE NEEDS HELP, BY ANSWERING QUESTIONS IN A CAREFUL AND THOUGHTFUL MANNER, BY HELPING EACH OTHER TO LISTEN IN CLASS AND BY ENCOURAGING ONE ANOTHER.

WE PROMISE TO CALL EACH OTHER WHEN POSSIBLE IN ORDER TO PROVIDE MISSED ASSIGNMENTS AND ADDITIONAL HELP.

WE WILL RECEIVE TEAM POINTS IF WE CAN IMPROVE, IF WE CAN BE BETTER TOGETHER THAN WE WERE APART.

WE PROMISE TO COOPERATE IN AN EFFECTIVE MANNER.

We especially promise to act as a **unique and valuable person** and to treat each member of our team as a **unique and valuable person**.

MY SIGNATURE _____

PARTNER SIGNATURE _____

TEACHER SIGNATURE _____

CAROLINA TEAMS

WE AGREE TO HELP EACH OTHER TO HAVE MAXIMUM SUCCESS BY LISTENING PATIENTLY TO ONE ANOTHER'S QUESTIONS, BY ASKING EACH OTHER FOR HELP, BY ASKING IF SOMEONE NEEDS HELP, BY ANSWERING QUESTIONS IN A CAREFUL AND THOUGHTFUL MANNER, BY HELPING EACH OTHER TO LISTEN IN CLASS AND BY ENCOURAGING ONE ANOTHER.

WE PROMISE TO CALL EACH OTHER WHEN POSSIBLE IN ORDER TO PROVIDE MISSED ASSIGNMENTS AND ADDITIONAL HELP.

WE WILL RECEIVE TEAM POINTS IF WE CAN IMPROVE, IF WE CAN BE BETTER TOGETHER THAN WE WERE APART.

WE PROMISE TO COOPERATE IN AN EFFECTIVE MANNER.

We especially promise to act as a **unique and valuable person** and to treat each member of our team as a **unique and valuable person.**

MY SIGNATURE _____

PARTNER SIGNATURE _____

PARTNER SIGNATURE _____

PARTNER SIGNATURE _____

ONE PERSON HAS TO TAKE ON THE RESPONSIBILITY TO MAKE SURE THE ENTIRE GROUP IS ON TASK. THIS PERSON IS YOUR **ENFORCER**. PICK ONE PERSON FOR THAT ROLE.

OUR ENFORCER IS _____

Engaging Students Using Cooperative Learning, John Strebe © Taylor & Francis

CAROLINA TEAMS IMPACT SHEET
(BONUS Points)

In order for you to have the greatest success in this class you need to CAREFULLY select one or two people who can have a positive impact on you and whom you can impact in a positive manner.

Get together with the person(s) you have selected and have them <u>initial</u> each of the following. You will initial their sheets as well as your own. Placing your initials in a blank means you and your partner(s) agree to do each of the activities described.

SELECT ONLY PEOPLE WHO CAN DO EACH OF THESE THINGS WITH YOU!

	My Initials	Partner's Initials	Second Partner's
We will <u>teach</u> each other.	_____	_____	_____
We will <u>learn</u> from each other.	_____	_____	_____
We will help each other to <u>pay attention</u> in class.	_____	_____	_____
We will <u>encourage</u> each other to do <u>homework</u>.	_____	_____	_____
We will strive for EXCELLENCE.	_____	_____	_____
Where possible, we will help each other <u>outside</u> class.	_____	_____	_____
We will earn <u>3 points</u> on our grade every time we **equal or beat** our target.	_____	_____	_____

MY NAME _____

MY PARTNER _____

SECOND PARTNER _____

When using Carolina Pairs and Teams either **Think-Pair-Share** or **Think-Pair-Square-Share** should be used in the teaching process, resulting in the necessary interaction for effective cooperative learning. Think-Pair-Square-Share serves as a vehicle for positive interaction and the bonus grade points provide the incentive.

The learning model described on these pages is certainly not perfect and needs improvements. It is also best used when *adapted and fitted* to the needs of a particular class or subject area. Hopefully, the user of Carolina Pairs/Teams will make the necessary changes, resulting in much benefit for both students and teachers.

A key decision needs to be made by anyone who chooses to use the Carolina system. *How important is cooperation?* How vital is the learning of skills that are necessary in having a positive impact on another person? My hope is that many will decide that these skills are important enough to be quantified and reflected in the computation of grades.

Using Carolina Pairs and Teams Without the Bonus Points

Objections to the adding of bonus points to grades are legitimate and should be carefully considered. In many classes I have used Carolina Teams and emphasized team competition but did not use the bonus point concept. I was better able to omit the use of bonus points as I refined my skills at getting students to cooperate effectively. I still used team competition with the team improvement points calculated as explained. If I were using Carolina for the first time, I would use bonus points, but they are not essential.

Rewarding teams or pairs for improvement becomes very important especially if bonus points are not used. Announcing to the class which groups had the greatest improvement results in "High 5's" and other celebrations. It is also important to recognize the group(s) that had the highest scoring average on the quiz. Lower achieving students have the most room to improve. Teams that are composed of very high achieving students do not have much room to improve and are at a distinct disadvantage to be the most improved.

It is important to award at least two champions instead of one, those that improved the most and those with the highest raw score on the evaluation. Some champions are those teams with the highest competition points score and other champions are the teams with the highest grades. Multiple champions increase the chances for winning, helping to create a more positive environment. Teams or pairs that improve the most or score the highest can be rewarded in a number of ways as determined by the teacher, such as having their pictures on a Wall of Fame.

Students immediately recognize the fairness of computing improvement points, eliminating the possibility of a "loaded" or weighted team that would never lose. Everyone has a chance to win. Students who understand the concept have responded with "Brilliant!" or with "We love that!"

The learning structure, **Carolina Pairs and Teams** resulted from my desire to address the needs expressed by students and from the shared experiences of Robyn Bailey, who was a teacher for the Amherst County Schools in Virginia. Robyn and I share affection for South Carolina and thus the name for the bonus points/improvement system.

On the following pages are sample points sheets which I have used to record Carolina data. The first sheet displays examples of data required for two Carolina teams and one Carolina pair. One blank points sheet is supplied for the user's benefit.

Carolina

Students	TGT	Q1	Q2	TGT2	Q3	Q4	TGT3	Q5	Q6	TGT4	Q7	Q8	TGT5	A
														1
														2
														3
														4
														5
														6
														7
														8
														9
														10
														11
														12
														13
														14
														15
														16
														17
														18
														19
														20
														21
														22
														23
														24
														25
														26
														27
														28
														29
														30
														31
														32

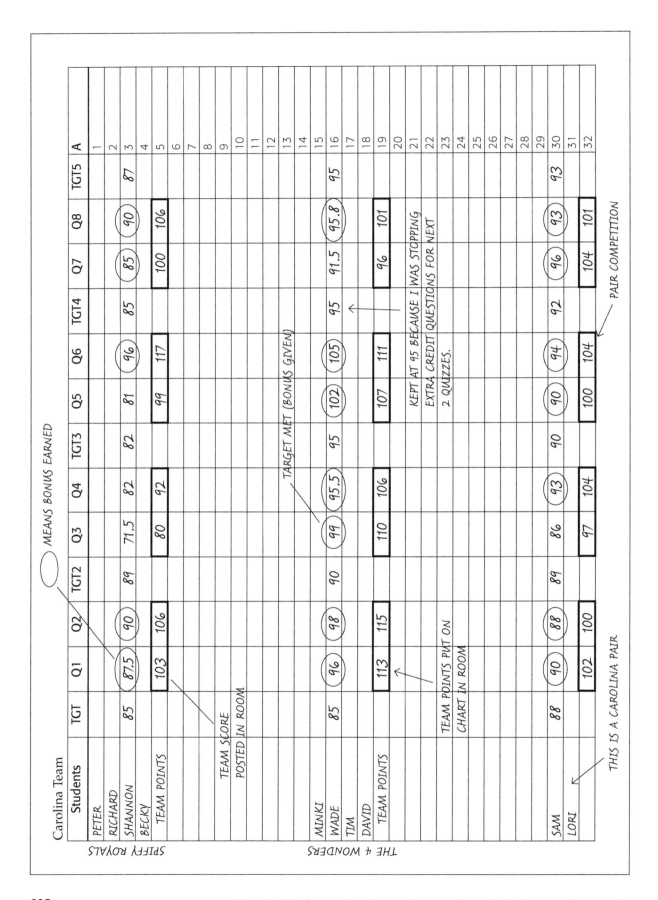

Engaging Students Using Cooperative Learning, John Strebe © Taylor & Francis

Chapter 10

Additional Teambuilders

Additional Team Builders

A team builder I sometimes use is called **Personal Share Pairs**. It is a great way for the kids to get to know each other, for the teacher to know the students and the students to know the teacher. Students got to know me because I always modeled the activity for my students. Some even became convinced that I was a human being, eating real food, paying bills and living life in the real world. Sometimes we teachers appear to our students as alien type creatures visiting from the Teacher Planet. Accepting us as genuine and authentic people may even convince them of the relevancy of the content that we are teaching them.

Personal Share Pairs

Students sit in their cooperative teams which range in size from 3 to 5 and are asked to observe, while the teacher models the activity. The teacher writes on the board or on newsprint a T chart divided into 2 columns labeled LIKES and DISLIKES. The teacher's name is written at the top of the chart. A student is asked to be the timekeeper and signal when a minute has passed. When the class hollers "Go!," the teacher writes as many personal likes and dislikes as time permits, probably stretching the minute a bit. The result looks something like this:

John Strebe

Likes	Dislikes
Wife	Rudeness
Kids	Bad Driving
Garden	Weeds
Basketball	Losing
Orioles	Intense Neatness
Golf	Whining
Romantic Movies	Snowmen (a golf term)
Neatness	Broken Machines
USC	
Celtics	

Now the teacher asks the students to make a T-chart on a piece of their own paper, writing or printing neatly their likes and dislikes. Several minutes are given for everyone to complete the listings. Next, the students are asked to think about other interesting preferences. One option is to have the students put a capital H (for *historical*) at the bottom of the lists and write the name of a person who is famous but who is no longer alive, someone with whom the student would like to spend a day as in a quantum leap of time.

Next the student places a capital N (for *now*) under the H and lists the name of a person who is famous and is still living with whom the student would enjoy spending 24 hours. Typically, names of athletes, war heroes, inventors, Hollywood stars, artists, leaders of movements, authors, musicians or musical groups characterize the students' responses. Sometimes an appropriate question to have students *think* about is, "What would you hope to gain from being with that person for a day?"

Under the N students could be asked to write a capital P (for purpose) and briefly describe their purpose in life. Sometimes this evokes an interesting discussion about purpose, citing examples and relating that the response today could very well change next week. The students may go back and add information as time permits. At this point the activity is done in **Respect Mode**, each student working alone and no student-to-student sharing allowed.

At this time students are asked to stop writing and focus on the teacher's list while in **Think Mode**, thinking about several questions that could be asked about the teacher's various likes and dislikes. Students pair up and share their questions with their partners while in **Pair Mode**, after which they raise hands and in rapid fire fashion ask the teacher about likes and dislikes. For example, "What kinds of things do you grow?" or "What is the difference between neatness and intense neatness?" or "What's this about snowmen?" This part of the activity is fun for everyone and helps students to feel closer to their teacher as well as understand that teachers are human too. Of course, the teacher reserves the right to refrain from answering certain questions. After a while, it is the students' turn to read each other's lists and ask questions. Remember, the purpose for this activity is for students to know each other better, lower the barriers to conversation and lessen biases so they will work together more effectively with the subject matter being taught.

A procedure to do this personal sharing in a team is described below:

First Sharing

Teams of 4: Your partner is the person opposite you. When the signal is given, exchange papers, BRIEFLY STARE AT YOUR PARTNER, READ YOUR PARTNER'S PAPER, AND TAKE TURNS ASKING AND ANSWERING QUESTIONS ABOUT EACH OTHER. Students also reserve the right not to answer certain questions.

Teams of 5: Two people are "twins" and function as one person. They exchange both of their papers with the person opposite them, while the other pair exchanges papers. The set of CAPITALIZED instructions above are followed. The one person matched with the twins must read 2 papers and question 2 people at the same time. The twins read about and question one person.

Teams of 3: Each person is assigned a number, using the numbers 1, 2 and 3. When the signal is given, #1's paper is given to #'s 2 and 3, while 2 and 3 keep their papers. The capitalized instructions are followed as #'s 2 and 3 read about #1 while #1 sits and waits to answer questions.

The teacher can walk around the room, listening to conversation, learning about the students and assisting students in asking questions. After a period of time students return to **Think Mode** and are encouraged to **reflect** on what has just been learned about this person, about how very special their partner is, after which they express thanks for the sharing, perhaps even shaking hands. Students get their own papers back.

Second Sharing

Teams of 4: New partner is the person next to you. Papers are exchanged.

Teams of 5: Two non-twins change seats to help conversation for twins and new partner. Papers are exchanged.

Teams of 3: #2 will give paper to #'s 3 and 1 who keep their own papers

Now the capitalized instructions are followed. Then **Reflect** again on the uniqueness of this person and express **Thanks**.

The students get their own papers back for the final exchange.

Final Sharing

Teams of 4: Two people on one side of the group switch seats. New partner is opposite you.

Teams of 5: Twins stay put and their next partner switches seats to be close to them.

Teams of 3: #3 gives paper to #2 and 1. Exchanges occur and the instructions are followed.

Perhaps all papers can be collected by one person in each group and given to the teacher for some enjoyable private reading. Generally, after this activity has been completed the members of teams feel much closer to each other and group efficiency is vastly improved. Although the extended block provides sufficient time for this activity as well as significant subject matter study, an attractive option is to divide the activity into segments and stretch the process over several days. Often the middle of a 90-minute block is a profitable time to complete a segment, providing an educational interrupter.

In some classes, students are not eager to write about themselves on totally blank paper. Prepared sheets can be used for the students to complete the information, and then using those sheets the instructions provided above can be followed. Three examples of prepared sheets are included here after the diagram describing the activity.

Provided on the next page are visual representations of how this activity is performed.

PERSONAL SHARE PAIRS

(Arrows indicate direction of paper passing.)

(Each row describes one step of the activity.)

TEAM OF 5	**TEAM OF 4**	**TEAM OF 3**
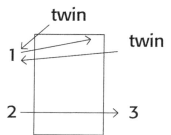	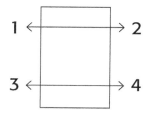	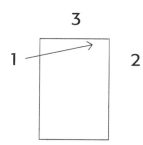
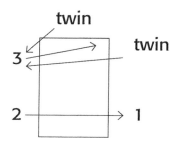		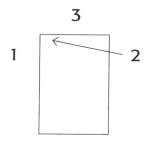
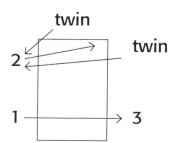	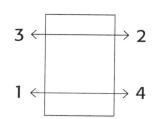	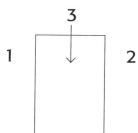

NAME _____ TEAM # _____

Favorite color is _____

Favorite musical group/singer _____

Hobbies or freetime activities _____

_____

_____

_____

Places I like to go _____

_____

I am good at this _____

I am bad at this _____

My future career hopes _____

A great summer vacation is _____

I am living for this purpose _____

_____

_____

Favorite foods _____

Person(s) I admire most in the world _____

_____

_____

WHO I AM

NAME _____

Favorite things (colors, foods, places to go, things to do, tv shows, cars hobbies, movies, music, etc.)

Things I don't like

What I like to do in summer

My future hopes

The person(s) alive now or who lived in the past whom I most admire

Engaging Students Using Cooperative Learning, John Strebe © Taylor & Francis

NAME _____

Colleges of interest   Possible college majors

1.

2.

3.

4.

What do you hope to be doing 15 years from now?
(Career, family , lifestyle, etc.)

What would be something a person could do that would really make a difference in the world—something worthwhile?

What countries would you most like to visit? Why?

If you were principal of our school what would you do to help us be better?

WHO I AM

NAME

BIRTHPLACE

BIRTH MONTH AND DAY(LIKE JAN 15)

PLACES I HAVE VISITED

THINGS I LOVE

Engaging Students Using Cooperative Learning, John Strebe © Taylor & Francis

WHO I AM

NAME

BIRTHPLACE

BIRTH MONTH AND DAY(LIKE JAN 15)

FAMOUS PEOPLE I ADMIRE

(BOTH FROM HISTORY AND STILL LIVING)

Sometimes students do not prefer writing or are unable to write. Making a **Team Collage** generates similar sharing as **Personal Share Pairs** and requires no writing. **Team Collage** can also take the place of the **Things In Common** team building activity.

Team Collage

Sometimes it is beneficial to create a visual object to help with team identification. The Team Collage can be very effective in helping individuals to feel a sense of belonging to a particular team. Creating the collage can help a team develop team spirit, especially if the project is completed with significant help from each student. The end product needs to be something "we" produced.

Supply students with magazines, safety scissors, a glue stick and a poster board. It is advisable to approve magazines brought in by the students. The poster board should be divided into sections, one for each team member. Each student cuts out pictures that represent favorite things and glues them to one particular section. The poster will have pictures of cars, celebrities, food, clothes, jewelry, video games—anything a kid might like. On the other side of the poster can appear the team name. With the team name can be a team design or team picture or drawing. Put a metal grommet in each, and hang the posters from the ceiling over the team location. The posters could be laminated. **Circle of Knowledge** can be used to allow each team member to share facts about the selected pictures within a team, building the team into a cohesive unit.

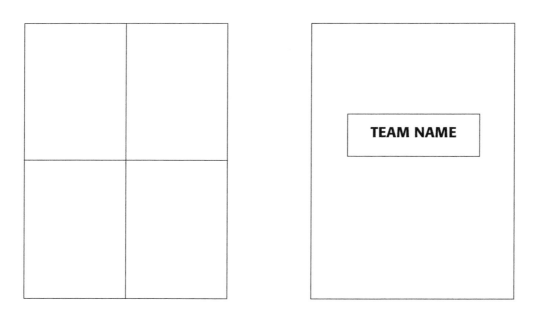

Alphabetic Foods

Students love competition, something which can be used to do effective team building. A fun activity that encourages students to interact at a high level is Alphabetic Foods. It can be fun and controversial. Use it to pull the kids together.

The students should be arranged in teams or pairs for this activity. Erase-and-wipe boards can be distributed, one per team.

Think/Pair/Team/Share will be used to begin a listing of alphabetic foods. In **Think Mode** the students each think of a food name beginning with the letter "A." The board writer interviews the team, helping the team to choose one "A" food as their team food. The single food name is written on the erase-and-wipe board. At a given signal, all boards are displayed for the entire class to see. One person is chosen from each team to write on a sheet of paper the entire alphabet, the letters written in a column, one letter per line. The team "A" food is written on the first line. The entire process is repeated for a "B" food. Do not go on to other letters.

The boards are erased and put away as the entire team leans toward the foods paper and one food name for each letter of the alphabet is written on the paper. Any food will do and this list should be created as quickly as possible. Do not vote on team foods. What is important is to get a food for each letter. Team members can suggest the names in any order as they come to mind. The environment is very noisy and busy. This process continues until each team has 26 food names listed on the team paper. Teams should be encouraged to be creative with the more difficult letters. Spelling does not count, except for the first letter.

Once the lists are completed the teams should celebrate with a "Strebe High 1" (see Chapter 3) and then begin to memorize their lists so that each team member could correctly respond with a food name for a requested letter. In other words, if the teacher said "C," then every student could write the name of a food beginning with the letter C.

After a few minutes, the team food lists are put away, out of sight. Another member of the team is selected to take out a piece of paper and make another columnar listing of the alphabet, letters only. The team name should be written on the top of that paper.

At a given signal a competitive **roundtable** activity will begin by using this paper to make a list of foods. The rules are as follows:

1. Each person writes a food and then passes the paper to the next person on the team.(Write neatly or print.)

2. The foods must be written in alphabetic order. No letters skipped.

3. The foods do *not* have to be from the team's generated list.

4. The team may not talk, lip sync, write notes, skywrite or provide help to a team-mate who may be struggling.

5. The team may *pantomime* any food for a person who becomes stuck. Remember, no talking!

6. A person who simply cannot think of a particular food may write "SHUCKS" next to the troubling letter and roundtable the paper. "SHUCKS" merely gives the team permission to go on, but will count as a missed letter at the end of the

activity. Remember, there is a time limit and at some point the "SHUCKS" answer may need to be used. Even though it will not count, it allows the next person to go on to the next letter.

7. Teams celebrate quietly when lists are completed using a whispered "Strebe High 1" or a celebration of the team's creation.

To summarize, no communication is allowed, except for a pantomime when a team member needs help. Foods must be supplied in alphabetic order and no letters skipped, no people may be skipped and the foods do **not** have to be from the team list. The list was created to cause people to begin thinking about food names. If someone cannot think of a food, time should be taken to think, watch the pantomimes from the team, and if still unsuccessful, the student should write "SHUCKS." No one may talk to anyone at any time during this activity.

When all the teams are finished, the lists are exchanged between teams. The teams must now decide whether or not each entry is the name of a food. Teams should place a check by an approved food name or a "?" by a nonapproved food name. If there is any doubt about the entry being a legitimate food, put a "?" If even one person thinks the entry is not a food, place a "?" During this time **no defense** of an entry may be stated; only a clarification of the spelling is allowed.

Once each team is finished the consensus process, **Circle of Knowledge** from team to team is used to bring all questions("?") before the class. The food name is read out loud; the class thinks quietly—no defense is allowed at all; each team leans toward the center of the team, discussing the questioned food name and consensus is reached. The teacher says, "Let's vote." If teams think the proposed food name is a legitimate food, the team gives the "thumbs up" signal. If the team believes that the food name is not a food, they holler the sound "WAAAH!" It requires more than half of the teams to holler "WAAAH!" for a food name to be scratched. Remember, no defense of any "food" is allowed at any time. Sometimes a legitimate food will be rejected by the class. After the activity has been completed a discussion about the difference between opinion and truth can be valuable.

After all questions have been voted on, teams are awarded one point for each acceptable food name and the team scores are displayed. Remember, "SHUCKS" earns no points. Winning teams may be rewarded in any appropriate manner.

The students have depended on each other for team performance, emphasizing the importance of each student mastering a skill. A team should have success only when every member of the team has success.

If time is a concern, prepare a sheet with some of the letters already written in a column, perhaps letters like A, B, C, D, E, F, G, K, M, O, Q, S, V, X and Z. Using an abbreviated list of letters can allow the activity to be completed in much less time. The benefits remain the same.

A Competitive Cooperative Game

When I adopted a different perspective on the classroom, emphasizing students working together and engaging each other around the subject matter, an entire new world opened up for me and creating for the classroom became the norm. One day a "blind squirrel" found an acorn and an intensely competitive game came to my mind, a structure to be used to review for a quiz. It is called Cry For Help.

Cry for Help

Cry For Help is a spirited cooperative game that can be great fun for a class and an effective tool for student learning. The game has been played in elementary, middle and high school, and since it is set in a very competitive environment, care should be taken to ensure a positive experience for everyone.

Once the teacher has decided that the game will be played, the class should be informed to provide for adequate preparatory study time. This may mean 10 minutes, overnight or a week to get ready, depending on the nature and extent of the academic material to be reviewed.

The game is played using existing teams or with teams created just for the competition. If the classroom is structured in learning pairs, the combination of two pairs could form a competition team. In any case, teams should be composed of 3 to 5 people. Each team should "number off" from 1 to 5 or if no team exceeds 4 members, from 1 to 4. Smaller teams will require one or two people to have 2 numbers. For example, if the same class has a 5-member team and a 3-member team, then 2 people in the 3-member team will be assigned one number from 1 to 3 and the number 4 or the number 5, respectively. These numbers designate a "batting order" once the competition begins.

Team response areas must be identified, one for each team, somewhere in the classroom. Newsprint can be taped to the wall or use a portion of the blackboard designated for a particular team. The team name or identifying team number is placed on the newsprint or on the board. Team response centers should be located a distance from the team to discourage verbal sharing of answers, but close enough so the team can read the team responses. Each team needs a magic marker or a piece of chalk.

From each team, batter #1 goes to the team response area, writes a given problem on the newsprint, while each team member writes the problem in his or her notebook. Problems may be given orally, on an overhead or in writing. A review sheet can be cut into many individual pieces and each piece distributed by the batter to the team prior to reporting to the team response area. All students (including the batter) work the problem, writing the answer. Batter #1 may not look back at the team or at any other batter. The team members back at their desks may whisper together checking each other's work, but their batter is not allowed to communicate with anyone. Seated team members should speak quietly because the team response area near them is for another team, allowing for overhearing of the discussion.

If the batter gets help by looking at the team or at other batters, that is called a "Cry For Help." The problem may be worth 10 points to the team, but when a "Cry For Help" occurs, the problem is now worth only 8 points to the affected team. If a batter should complete the response, then the batter may rejoin the team at their desks to receive congratulations and enjoy quiet celebration.

If the team discovers that their batter made an error, they may accompany their batter back to the team response area, assisting the batter in correcting the response. However, this means that the problem is worth 8 rather than 10 points for that team. Teams may use several "Cries For Help" on the same problem without incurring additional point reduction. If the problem is never answered correctly, then the team earns 0 points for that problem. This encourages every member of the team to find a solution to the problem. The batter may initiate the help of the team, or if the batter is "stuck and stubborn," the team may initiate the help. At an appropriate time for each problem, the teacher could warn that only 20 seconds remain for that problem, then warn at 10 seconds indicating that this is a good time to "Cry" if needed.

After time for the first problem has expired, batter #2 then goes to the team response area; the problem's answer is provided for the entire class; batter #2 checks and records the score for the previous problem and waits for a new problem. Explanation to the class of the correct approach to the first problem is made at this time. Often, a student will explain using the displayed work. Emphasize to the class that *everyone works every problem*. Team members not batting do the problems in their notebooks. The competition proceeds from batter to batter and can last for 90-minutes. It is helpful to increase the worth of the problems as the time passes; this allows for teams that have fallen behind the opportunity to catch up. At the close of the class the cumulative score for each team is computed and appropriate rewards for top-performing teams are presented. All students now have review material and solutions to study for the coming test in their notes. Both the losing and the winning teams are better prepared for the coming test. Many students are now more aware of concepts which need further study.

Cry For Help provides extreme pressure on the individual student and reinforces the value of the team. After having played the game once, students tend to study more intensely in preparation for the next "Cry For Help" adventure. In fact, students have prepared more thoroughly for this game than for the actual test because peer pressure is huge here.

Some students will attempt to cheat by looking for help from other batters or from the team. Instead of saying, "You are cheating," the teacher who is carefully observing says, "That's a cry for help!" At that point, the team comes to the team response area to provide the much needed help. This can mean, say, that 45 points will be earned on a 50-point question, which is considerably better than 0 points for an incorrect response.

Adaptations of the game should be made to fit student needs, room arrangement and subject differences. Make the game fun for everyone.

Chapter 11
Myths/Questions

Myths

The weather report indicated that there was a chance for a snowfall around drive time tomorrow morning, but the storm may pass to the north of our city. All good teachers told their students to be sure to complete all homework tonight and definitely to wear pajamas inside out. According to legend this would guarantee the snowstorm closing schools. Of course, these are just myths and are fun to propagate and practice. Maybe they are not myths. I know a teacher who did no lesson plans the night before an approaching storm only to see the storm not materialize. The next day that teacher learned to "shoot from the hip" as the classes were taught.

Some myths can be extremely harmful and can damage good people as well as valuable ideas. Cooperative learning has been demonized by some folks, primarily through the repetition of untrue statements, myths about classroom collaboration. Learning to collaborate with others in order to accomplish a goal is the way good families and productive groups operate.

Unfortunately, well meaning people do make untrue statements about cooperative learning. These falsehoods can come from inaccurate perception or from observing cooperative learning that has been badly done.

I was having lunch with the participants in a workshop I was conducting when one of the participants expressed their fondness for cooperative learning because only one quiz from each team needed to be graded and that reduced the amount of work for the teacher. I almost fell off my chair and began to realize the need for sharing statements like these as the myths that they are, so we would not believe or practice them in our teaching. The list provided here are myths and not characteristics of an effective cooperative environment. Each of them is a comment I have heard teachers declare as true. Read them all and choose three to which you could most strongly react. For your benefit, write down your reactions to them. Think of facts which dispel all of these.

Green Cheese on the Moon and Other

Myths about cooperative learning:

- ♦ There is no lecture in cooperative learning. (Only the kids teach.)
- ♦ All groups are cooperative.
- ♦ One kid does all the work and the other 3 get "A's" too.
- ♦ Groups are always heterogeneous.

♦ Smart kids are always stuck teaching the others.

♦ Gifted kids get held back.

♦ Cooperative learning just "dumbs down" our classes.

♦ Anybody can do cooperative learning: it's easy.

♦ Noise is bad.

♦ Students don't need to learn how to work together.

♦ You can't be rigorous and do cooperative learning too.

♦ Don't ever put good friends together in the same group or pair.

♦ The teacher gets nothing back from the effort it takes to go cooperative.

♦ Cooperative learning is all or nothing. (Do it all the time or never.)

♦ Cooperative learning is the *only* way to go.

♦ I can't be the authority and cooperate too.

♦ I am too old to change!

♦ Good teachers do not need to try new ideas.

As you record your reactions to the above statements you will be less likely to have them be true of you and you will not only avoid them but you will be able to explain cooperative learning strategies to others more effectively.

One of the above statements motivates me to excellence. "I am too old to change" really bothers me. Someone asked me how long I planned to teach and my answer was that my goal would be to teach for 50 years. I genuinely believe that I need to be a better teacher my 50th year than I would have been during my 49th year. If this is not true, then I would have retired a year too late. Each year we have the privilege of having an impact on unique and valuable young people and we, who are called to this, will always seek to improve and do this more effectively. I hope there might be one idea, philosophy or strategy included in this book that will enable you to do this.

I challenge you as one who is called to teach, to rediscover, and keep your passion. Passion will motivate you to improve and rededicate yourself to this sacred calling. Do not forget that **You Are Unique and Valuable** and you can discover new ways to **Act Unique and Valuable** in and out of the classroom.

Commonly Asked Questions

Through the years I have been asked questions by teachers attending workshops I have been privileged to conduct. Some of the more frequently asked questions are below. Please do not accept my answers to them as absolute truth. My answers come from my own experience in the cooperative classroom and are the result of this very imperfect person's thinking. Perhaps both the questions and the answers will help you in your quest to have students learn cooperatively.

♦ **Do random teams work?**

Yes, especially if you are super blessed and can safely drive your car for 20 miles while blindfolded through a busy city. For the best chance at success, form teams carefully and on purpose as described in this book according to the students' **strengths** and **needs**.

♦ **Can I start this in the middle of a year after teaching another way all year?**

Yes, in fact should you use any of these strategies in the middle of a year it will, at the very least, freshen the learning environment. I know of at least one instance where a teacher began using these strategies 4th quarter in a class of seniors taking a course not required for graduation, a course offered the last period of the school day. At the close of the year she told me that using cooperative teams had "saved her class."

♦ **Do you ever split up a team or pair that is not having success?**

Yes, but as a last resort. I try to describe for a group how they can improve. I will tell a troubled team, "You are on probation." Sometimes the team will make the necessary changes. If the team continues to struggle, I can split them up, spreading them around the classroom. In this instance, some 5- or 3-member teams may result.

In the early years when I did not take the necessary time to select my teams, making team changes happened more frequently, but now that I take the time and care, dissolving a team is a rare occurrence.

♦ **Do you ever have a student who refuses to work with a group?**

Yes, but rarely. For the first 8 days or so all students have worked in various teams and pairs. Class has been positive and fun as the different groups interact, compete and engage. If a student strongly objects to the team placement, I would ask why and attempt to fix the problem. If the problem continues, I would ask the student to look around the room to see if there is a team which would be more appropriate. Then, I would ask that team if this new person could join them. In a most extreme case, the student might refuse all team membership. My response has been that the student must have a partner and it is me, the teacher. Of course, rewards are given for team performance and there will be none for this student. In addition, I have responsibilities to other students as well, and I will not always be available as a partner. I then ask the student to think about this and make a choice tomorrow. I go through these options slowly and in the final step it is the student who makes a choice.

♦ **Do you ever have a student with whom no other student will work?**

Once in a while this does occur. In that case I try to find two students who are some of my best teachers and who are most tolerant. I present to them the challenge of having success with this person, pointing out to them they will be with this person for at most 8 weeks and then they are done. They may have a similar experience in the real world on their first job and have the opportunity here in school to learn ways to adjust to this situation. Sometimes I am able to work with this unwanted person and effect some change. It is certainly true that when I have two students assist me in working with this student, there is a greater chance for success. This is a case where it is vital that something like, "We are all Unique and Valuable" is in place. After 8 weeks I can usually find two other students who have grown to the point where they can work with this person.

◆ **What if I have 32 students in a class. Will this work?**

My experience has been that not only does cooperative learning work with a large class, but it allows for more teaching and help as students teach and help each other. Taking the desks out of rows and arranging them into teams creates floor space. It is more difficult for students to "get lost" in a cooperative team class; their team members hold them accountable. In a class this size I would organize the teams into two divisions so there will be a champion in each division, doubling the number of winners in each competition. After a competition I can reorganize the divisions putting the two winners in the same division, guaranteeing at least one new winner in the next competition.

◆ **How often do you crown a team champion?**

Ideally, I like to crown a champion every five 90-minute periods or every ten 50-minute periods, usually after a quiz is given with individual accountability. After the champions have been crowned, all point totals are returned to 0 for the next competition and the teams remain the same.

◆ **Suppose I have only 7 students in a class. How could I use this approach?**

I would have three teams: two teams with 2 people and one team with 3 people. Only one division containing three teams would be required.

◆ **What do you do when a new student is assigned to your class?**

I greet the student warmly with a handshake and for the day have the student sit with a team that I know will be good at welcoming a new person. I ask the students in the team to explain how the class works.

The new student has the opportunity to engage with the team about our subject matter. At the close of class, I would give the new student a class syllabus. The next few days I would have the new student sit with various teams until I determine which team would provide the best placement. I might even ask the new student for some input. What is profitable is the welcoming of the new student by classmates and that this does not fall only on the teacher.

◆ **Other than points earned on tests and quizzes, how do teams earn competition points?**

Points are awarded for collaborative performance on practice sheets or team activities and for in class answers to "tough" questions. I also have given points to the team when a teammate asks a particularly incisive question or makes a wonderful statement of truth. These in-class points would be small compared to the points earned on a quiz. A teacher could award points for any quality performance of a team or member of a team such as making great decorative cuts of vegetables in a culinary arts class.

♦ **Are the team points on the scoreboard used to determine student grades?**
I do not use these points in the grade book primarily because they were earned as the result of collaboration. The team competition is used to encourage students to work hard for team glory and eventually for the love of learning and love of the subject. Giving group grades can endanger the cooperative climate and invites justified criticism. The only structure I use to reward students in the grade book is the Carolina system.

♦ **I am a "floater" and teach in 3 different rooms. Can the cooperative learning teaching structure be managed?**
Most definitely. I used the cooperative learning teaching structure while floating for 4 years. To be sure, there are challenges which must be confronted. Most important will be the collaboration between the room teacher and the floating teacher. We agreed that each of us would be responsible for arranging the desks for our own class and leave them that way for the next teacher. I taught my students to arrange the desks into teams as well as into pairs so they arranged the desks according to my instructions. Sometimes I was able to use a part of the wall for display, but when that was not possible, I would use "shower board" purchased and cut at a local building supply store. One board held the team names and points and another one held the Wall of Fame. These boards were conveniently stored behind a file cabinet and displayed during our class on a chalk tray.

♦ **Will the students become bored if 10 teachers use these strategies in our school?**
My experience has been that the kids do not become bored. Instead, their fun while learning is multiplied. Individual differences among teachers make strategies appear different in each classroom. As time goes on, the differences in application become even greater, truly making each classroom a unique learning environment. How interesting during the past when most instruction was done by teachers lecturing from the front, rarely did anyone have concern about the students' boredom. Our challenge is to adapt and create to make what we use fit our specific situation and to enable students to engage in learning at a high level.

♦ **Do you do team building only when new teams are formed?**
Sometimes team building needs to be revisited several weeks after a team has begun to work together. It is not something you do once and then put it away.

♦ **Will I have enough space to do this in my small room?**
My experience has been that rearranging the furniture into a cooperative setting actually created additional space. Reducing noise may be important in a small area. Teach students to whisper and to communicate with each other and with the teacher using erase-and-wipe boards and nonverbal cues.

♦ **My furniture is not appropriate for a cooperative classroom.**
For years I had my "own" room and furniture I loved. Becoming a floating teacher allowed me to experience various types of furniture.

The old style one-piece desk and chair style requires an organization where each writing area is pointed toward the center of the group. At least one desk is on an angle to allow all students to sit comfortably. Another arrangement puts the desks in a "wagon train" requiring the students to enter the seat from the outside of the circle. One of the rooms had heavy, long typing desks without the typewriters. Teams sat two behind two and the front two students turned around and worked on the desks of their teammates behind them. I have actually held cooperative classes in a typical school auditorium. **Team Building** and structured communication like **Think/Pair/Square/Share** are especially important in such a setting.

♦ **What if it does not go well the first time?**
If using a cooperative structure does meet all your expectations the first time, then be thankful. You have been blessed! When it does not go well, fix what went wrong and try again. You will continue to fix and try especially if you attempted a cooperative classroom because you believed that it was good for you and the students. You will get better and better until it becomes second nature. I even use aspects of cooperative learning when I am called upon to substitute for a fellow teacher.

♦ **Do all types of students do well with cooperative learning?**
My experience has been that they do. For years, two of my classes were made up of advanced placement or underclass gifted and talented students. Two other classes were populated with a majority who were learning disabled students. In both settings, the students eventually engaged with each other, learned to care about one another, celebrated learning and had academic success. I found greater success in the class of special education students beginning the year with teams of 2 students each and working our way into larger teams. In the advanced placement classes I observed a significant increase in student empathy. In both groups, positive peer pressure was a powerful tool.

♦ **How should I begin?**
I would advise to start small. Select a manageable structure like **Think/Pair/Share** and introduce that in a class where you think it has a good chance of working well. Refine it and use it again. Continue the process until you become confident. At that point, select another structure like **Respect/Defense/Consensus** worksheets and perfect it. At some point, select a class and form teams according to the students' strengths and needs and create cooperative teams. As you become increasingly skilled, use these structures in other classes. One valuable idea is to find another teacher who will attempt these things as well. As you observe each other teach and discuss what you have experienced, you can profitably coach each other. I was unwise and began with teams in two classes and it worked! How exciting to gain confidence and have all classes profit from cooperative concepts.

♦ **What if I decide nothing in this book is appropriate for me, but I am enthusiastic about the cooperative classroom model?**
The contents of this book are limited by the space and the insights of the author. Use the Internet to find other resources for cooperative learning. There are many and perhaps you will find exactly what you need or adapt what you find to you and your classroom. Create a cooperative structure that is new and fits your situation. This is exciting and renewing!

Conclusion

Making a Difference

My first teaching experience was in an inner-city high school where the schools were not desegregated. The students were wonderful people who were experiencing the good and the bad of the city and had come to get an education. Many of my students did not have a positive male role model in the home, a fact which began to shape my perception of the purpose I would serve at the school. A government sponsored program supplied resources for me to spend time with 10 first-year male students, taking them to athletic events, ice skating, bowling and picnics. As our relationship matured, I realized we needed a format that would allow us to talk about the major issues of their lives. My wife and I began to have the guys out to our house for a full course dinner once each week after which the young men and I had a "rap" session about some pertinent topic.

We discussed drugs, sex, marriage, fatherhood, race relations, academics, college and many other topics. Since my life was rooted on a strong spiritual base, we included Bible studies which dealt with all the topics we had previously talked about. I began to realize that the kids were learning more by observing my life with my wife than perhaps anything we discussed. That prompted weekends at our home, taking hikes along the river and day trips to various events.

I also realized that most of the kids did not have in their families a person who had gone on to professional training after high school. I discovered that some colleges provided college weekends for high school students to experience college life by staying in the dorms and going to classes. We arranged several of these trips to schools in different states, truly educational, since some of the students had never been out of their home state and some had never been outside of the city limits.

One trip was to a southern state, causing some apprehension among my kids who were all African Americans—this being the early 1970s. After much convincing, including affirming that we were not trying to "get the kids cut," about 15 kids piled into a large van and car and headed south. The educational value of this trip was great, going beyond academics. After stopping at a fast food place in North Carolina, one of my young men marveled that the white worker had treated him with respect, even saying, "Thank you, Sir." What these students learned on this trip was priceless!

After spending the weekend in the college dormitory, the students began to perceive themselves in a different way. They began to believe that they could attend college, opening new horizons for them.

The college experience was invaluable for the young students. In addition, the kids had opportunities to speak to a large group of residents at a female juvenile detention center as well as address male inmates in a "chain gang" facility. The kids shared about the spiritual growth they had been experiencing in their lives and challenged the listeners to set a new course for their lives.

My students were not the only ones who learned much. The people in my home church heard the kids speak at the church service on Sunday night. After the service, young people from the church asked if they could take these kids from a different culture and of a different race out with them to their evening hangouts. I gave my permission, followed by much prayer for the safety of everyone. This was perhaps the first time that either group of young people had ever been out socially with those of a different race. The next morning when everyone had returned safely, I thought about the changes in my students and the young people in my home church. In the days that followed I was to learn that some of the adults in the church had dramatically changed the way they thought about people. All this happened because I was called to teach! How fortunate was I?

On the trip home I reflected on the immense value this trip had been for my students and for the people they met in the south. We were able to take several more such trips with the students and not coincidentally, many of the kids went on to college. This past year I reunited with some of these students, now in their '50s, and was blessed to see them with their families and hear of the success in their lives. I said to my wife, "Could we have lived our lives in a more productive way." She answered, "Not at all!" We teachers can make a difference.

Everyone who has been called to teach could recount similar, yet different stories about the effects of caring for students. Many times we do not hear until years after the student has graduated about the difference we made. We all know the warmth that comes as we receive e-mails, letters and phone calls communicating appreciation like those listed below:

"You made history come alive for me."

"Thanks for helping me when I was a freshman. I could not have made it without you."

"Thanks for believing in me!"

"You taught me to never give up."

"I was stupid when I was in your class, but you cared and showed me a better way."

"Thanks for helping me out with my parents."

Teachers can have a tremendous impact beyond the classroom, but in order to be genuine and authentic, what goes on in the classroom should be powerful and of high quality. The needs of young people are varied, yet kids everywhere have needs and we teachers are in a position to respond to those needs in powerful ways in the classroom and out.

For me, the cooperative classroom provides the greatest opportunity to build relationships with my students, while studying rigorous academic material. The students seem more able in a cooperative setting to engage with each other about ideas, achieving a depth of learning that did not occur as readily in the recitation model classroom. *I, me and my* were replaced with *we, us and our*. The cooperative classroom became a place where we all could better grow as people, develop our character and advance intellectually. The classroom became more like family and a home for everyone. I encourage you as a passionate teacher to reflect on what you have read here and respond appropriately for you and your students.

What a privilege to enable students to catch a vision about the possibilities for their lives. We need to have passion for what we do. Some of us have forgotten, having been burned out by the system or the demands of the profession. Our passion needs to be rekindled, our passion for the subject we teach, for the students whom we teach and for the teaching itself. Every day we have the opportunity to impact kids for the good. If we can help one young person to grow, to not quit but to engage in life, what is that worth? It is beyond monetary value.

My hope is that something in this book will enable the reader to better respond to the needs of students. It has been a privilege to teach and it is with gratitude that I share these ideas.

Perhaps you agree with me that teaching is not a job, but a calling.

Bibliography

Dunn, R., & Dunn, K. (1978). *Teaching Students Through Their Individual Learning Styles: A Practical Approach.* Englewood Cliffs, NJ: Prentice Hall.

Johnson, D. W., Johnson, R. T., & Holubec, E. J. (1993). *Cooperation in the Classroom* (6th. ed.), Edina, MN: Interaction Book Co.

Kagan, S. (1995). *Classbuilding: Cooperative Learning Activities.* San Juan Capistrano, CA: Kagan Cooperative Learning.

Kagan, S., & Kagan, M. (1998). *Multiple Intelligences: The Complete MI Book.* San Clemente, CA: Kagan.

Lyman, F. (1987). *Think-Pair-Share: An Expanding Teaching Technique.* MAACIE,

Cooperative News 1, 1.

National Institute of Environmental Health Sciences, http://kids.niehs.nih.gov/braint-pics.htm

Slavin, R. E. (1995). *Cooperative Learning: Theory, Research and Practice* (2nd. ed),

Appendix

Included in the Appendix are reproducible expressions of the cooperative classroom's basic philosophy. In addition are sample role cards for the Enforcer or Sheriff. Copies of these can be distributed to the students where appropriate.

YOU ARE

UNIQUE

AND

VALUABLE

THEREFORE
ACT

UNIQUE

AND

VALUABLE

CHOICES HAVE CONSEQUENCES,

SO

MAKE WISE

CHOICES

THE
ENFORCER

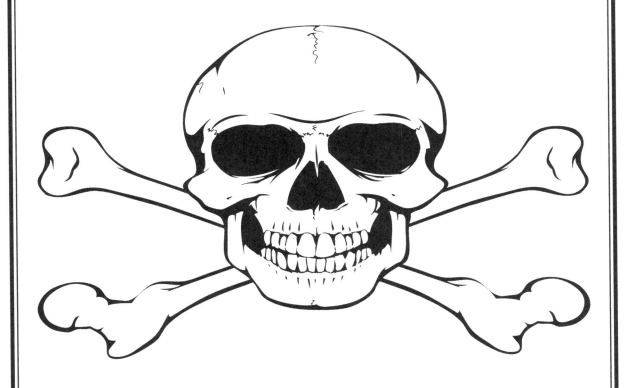

The Enforcer

THE
SHERIFF

For Product Safety Concerns and Information please contact
our EU representative GPSR@taylorandfrancis.com Taylor & Francis
Verlag GmbH, Kaufingerstraße 24, 80331 München, Germany

T - #0073 - 090625 - C0 - 276/216/10 - PB - 9781138302631 - Gloss Lamination